Images 30 is dedicated to

Michael Bramman
(1934 - 2006)

Illustrator and, from 2001 - 2005,
AOI Chairman

Images 30 is the all
new anniversary edition
of Images, the UK's
only jury-selected
illustration annual.
With an eye catching
cover design, revised
structure, features such
as the Critic's Award
and introducing the
New Talent section
which showcases the
best of today's students,
it justifies its position as
the essential publication
for leading industry
professionals as well
as academics, students
and practitioners.

Images 30

Edited and published by
The Association of Illustrators
2nd Floor, Back Building
150 Curtain Road
London
EC2A 3AT

Tel. +44 (0)20 7613 4328
Fax +44 (0)20 7613 4417
info@theaoi.com
www.theaoi.com

Copyright © The Association of Illustrators, London 2006

Portrait of Helen Osbourne on page 20 by Lucinda Rogers
Portrait of Steven Appleby on page 32 by Jon Barraclough

ISBN 0 9515448 88

Production in Hong Kong by
Hong Kong Graphics and Printing Ltd
Tel: (852) 2976 0289
Fax: (852) 2976 0292

The Association of Illustrators

AOI Volunteer Council of Management
Paul Bowman, Michael Bramman, Russell Cobb, Adam Graff,
Rod Hunt, Simon Pemberton, Louise Weir

AOI Chair
Russell Cobb

AOI Deputy Chair
Rod Hunt

Company Secretary
Michael Bramman

AOI Images Committee
Stephanie Alexander, Silvia Baumgart, Russell Cobb,
Stella Di Meo, Adam Graff, Rod Hunt, Sabine Reimer

Advisors
Stephanie Alexander, Alison Branagan, Stuart Briers,
Andrew Coningsby, Tamlyn Francis, Ruth Gladwin, Elliot Haag,
Anna Hallam, Chris Haughton, Tony Healey, Frazer Hudson,
Christine Jopling, Alison Lang, Samantha Lewis, Robert Lands,
Simon Stern, Fig Taylor, Caroline Thompson, Jimmy Turrell,
Adrian Valencia, Bee Willey, Jo Young

Manager
Silvia Baumgart
silvia@theaoi.com

Exhibitions and Events Co-ordinator
Stella Di Meo
events@theaoi.com

Images Co-ordinator
Sabine Reimer
images@theaoi.com

Publications/Membership Co-ordinator
Derek Brazell
derek@theaoi.com

Membership Co-ordinator
Helen Carmichael
info@theaoi.com

Finance Officer
Ian Veacock BA(Hons) FCCA
finance@theaoi.com

Press and Marketing Assistant
Dorothee Dines
press@theaoi.com

Book Design
Simon Sharville
www.simonsharville.co.uk

Patrons:

Glen Baxter

Peter Blake

Quentin Blake

Raymond Briggs

Chloe Cheese

Carolyn Gowdy

Brian Grimwood

John Hegarty

David Hughes

Shirley Hughes

Sue Huntley

Mick Inkpen

Donna Muir

Ian Pollock

Gary Powell

Tony Ross

Ronald Searle

Paul Slater

Ralph Steadman

Simon Stern

Peter Till

Janet Woolley

Contents

About the **AOI**

The Association of Illustrators was established in 1973 to advance and protect illustrators' rights and is a non-profit making trade association dedicated to its members' professional interests and the promotion of contemporary illustration. As the only body to represent illustrators and campaign for their rights in the UK, the AOI has successfully increased the standing of illustration as a profession and improved the commercial and ethical conditions of employment for illustrators. On behalf of its members and with their continued support, the AOI can achieve goals that it would be difficult or impossible for creators to attempt alone.

The AOI provides a voice for professional illustrators and by weight of numbers and expertise is able to enforce the rights of freelance illustrators at every stage of their careers. The AOI not only enables individual illustrators to deal with today's market, it lobbies parliament to change legislation through the Creators Rights Alliance and the British Copyright Council. AOI liaises with national and international organisations, art buyers, agents and illustrators over industry problems and campaigns against unfair contracts and terms of trade.

Campaigning and Net-working
The AOI is responsible for establishing the right for illustrators to retain ownership of their artwork and helped to establish the secondary rights arm of the Designers and Artists Copyright Society (DACS), the UK visual arts collecting society. In addition, it is a member of the Creators Rights Alliance (CRA), the British Copyright Council (BCC) and a founder member of the European Illustrators Forum (EIF).

Retaining of artwork
Each commission, while serving the needs of the brief, generates an original. Its lifetime in print will contribute to the world's greatest, most accessible and diverse wall-less art gallery. Therefore, it is important that the artist is aware of the value of the original and should always retain ownership of the original artwork. Stickers are available from the AOI ensuring that artwork is returned to the illustrator.

Design and Artists Copyright Society (DACS)
DACS is a not-for-profit membership based organisation representing various creators, including illustrators. They provide a range of licensing services for copyright consumers seeking to license the individual rights of an artist. Licenses for secondary uses of artistic works such as photocopying and television use are administered under collective licensing schemes on behalf of all visual creators. DACS negotiates a share of revenue from these schemes and distributes payments through their Payback service. DACS has been distributing this revenue since 1999, and has seen massive growth in licensing revenue pay-outs and in the numbers of visual creators benefiting since then. The AOI helped to establish the secondary rights arm of DACS and our patron Simon Stern sits on their board. AOI also distributes the DACS application form to members each year. For further information please visit www.dacs.org.uk

The British Copyright Council
The British Copyright Council (BCC) was established in 1965 and is a national consultative and advisory body representing organisations of copyright owners and performers and others interested in copyright in the UK.

It functions principally as a liaison committee for its member associations, providing them with a forum for the discussion of matters of copyright interest. It also lobbies the British Government, the European Commission and Parliament and international bodies such as the World Intellectual Property Organisation on matters of copyright and related issues. The BCC itself is a very small operation, run on a shoestring budget, with no formal constitution but it does represent large professional associations and unions, for example, the Publishers' Association, the Musicians' Union, the MCPS/PRS Alliance and the AOI. It is the only organisation of its type in the UK. Similar bodies in other countries were initiated, and are largely funded, by the relevant government department (e.g. the Australian Copyright Council), but this is not the case in the UK, although the BCC speaks with considerable authority on copyright issues and is frequently consulted by government. For further information please visit: www.britishcopyright.org

Creators Rights Alliance (CRA)
CRA was formed in 2001 and is now a group of seventeen organisations, comprising approximately 120,000 individual copyright creators and content providers working throughout the UK media marketplace. The CRA consists of such organisations as the Musicians Union, the National Union of Journalists, the Association of Photographers and the Society of Authors amongst others, as well as the AOI. The aim of the Alliance is to defend its members interests against abuses of creators' rights in all media, including magazine and newspaper publishing and broadcasting. The problems faced by illustrators are shared across a whole range of creative industries. The lack of equality between individual sole trader, freelance creators, and huge publishing multinationals complete with teams of lawyers has never been more apparent. These two parties are seen as equally equipped to negotiate with one another under the eyes of the law, but recent events have shown that the playing field is anything but level.

As a part of the CRA, the AOI is now able to lobby parliament for changes in the law, aligning UK law more closely with those of our European neighbours who are widely seen as more creator friendly. We regularly respond, as part of the CRA, to government led reviews of professional conduct and copyright legislation such as the Culture Media and Sports Committee's inquiry on New Media and the Creative Industries.

European Illustrators Forum (EIF)
Founded in 2003, the European Illustrators Forum now has 19 member associations in Europe. Its aim is to lobby the European Parliament for better legislation for creative people, create awareness of illustration on an international level and reach illustrators that are not yet associated with trade organisations. Through joint ventures, members can for example tour exhibitions Europe wide or organise high profile conferences funded by the European Union. It is important for each association to be part of a wider network to gain more political force and greater recognition of issues related to illustration. The EIF is currently working on a basic licence agreement valid throughout the European Union and a European conference on the scale of ICON in the US. Member representatives meet regularly at the Bologna Children's Book Fair in March and at the Frankfurt Book Fair in October.

Information and Support Services
In the past year, the AOI has continued to improve services to its members. Members of the AOI not only sustain campaigning and networking to improve working conditions for all they benefit personally from AOI services.

Members stay informed with our wide range of events and seminars. Varoom magazine, UP info poster and the Despatch newsletter keep members and subscribers up to date with events, practice and developments in the industry. Members receive up to 50% off our topical range of events and forums, with themes ranging from children's books, to self-promotion, pricing and up-to-the-minute industry debates.

Resources to help illustrators succeed
Members receive large discounts on essential publications, including the Images annual, Rights - The Illustrator's Guide to Professional Practice, The Big Picture - The Illustrator's Guide to a Professional Career and our range of targeted directory listings of illustration commissioners. Members of the AOI can receive discounts in art shops around the country.

They have access to essential professional and business advice including free dedicated hotline for legal, ethical and pricing advice, discounted consultations with our pool of industry specialists including business advisors, a life coach, chartered accountant and portfolio consultants.

Resources to help commissioners succeed
The AOI's Guide to Commissioning Illustration will save time and money by guiding you safely through all pitfalls of the commissioning process – even the most experienced might still learn something. Commissioners receive Images - the only jury-selected source book in the UK - free of charge when registering on the AOI's website. Our online portfolios give you access to more than 7000 classified images and the artist's contact details at a click.

Promotion
Members can receive substantial discounts on the AOI's online portfolios and our 'Images' competition and exhibition, showcasing the best of British contemporary illustration. The annual is the only jury-selected source book, despatched to over 4000 prominent commissioners of illustration.

Inspiration
Talks with leading illustrators, industry debates and discounted entry to competitions and exhibitions. Members receive a free subscription to Varoom, a full colour magazine the UK's creative industry has been waiting for. Varoom is a sumptuous celebration of 'made' images. Varoom features interviews with leading illustrators and image-makers as well as in-depth articles on different aspects and themes of contemporary illustration. It's stimulating line-up of interviews, profiles, history and polemic make Varoom essential reading for everyone interested in visual communication.

Contact
To request further information or a membership application form please telephone +44 (0)20 7613 4328

Foreword by **Russell Cobb**

Welcome to the 30th Anniversary edition of Images. New, improved and better than ever (well, I would say that, wouldn't I?)

It's true, though, that at the age of 30 Images is in its prime. It's still the only UK jury-selected awards book in Britain. It's still the first port of call for anyone looking for the very best in illustration. And it continues to inspire and excite, and to act as an important historical document for the future.

But times are changing, and it's vital we don't rest on our laurels. That's why in my first year as chairman I've instigated some important new initiatives.

We've launched the new magazine VAROOM, to raise the profile of illustration and illustrators.

We've moved to new, larger premises, and hired more staff.

We've been improving and expanding our website, to better service members' interests (our membership has doubled in the past ten years).

We've also - and this is a subject dear to all our hearts – implemented a pricing survey as the first step in preventing a further erosion of fees.

As illustrators, we are all individuals, and working alone is what many of us are used to. At the same time, we can all benefit from acting as a group sometimes. The AOI can, and should, be a rallying point for all of us, and a forum for representing our interests. That's why the AOI will continue to be proactive, lobbying parliament through groups such as the Creative Rights Alliance and the British Copyright Council. And why it will continue to build international

relationships and to raise awareness of, and engage with, new media, new technologies and new opportunities for our members.

I'm proud to have been fortunate to have had my work appear in past Images annuals. But I'm even prouder to have been asked to serve as Chairman for 2006.

I couldn't have achieved anything in my chairmanship without the fantastic support of the AOI office team and the AOI Council. I would like to thank in particular our Deputy Chairman Rod Hunt for his ongoing support and assistance during my first year and our Manager Silvia Baumgart for her dedication and professionalism.

I'd also like to thank the many organisations and individuals who contribute to the success of the Images exhibition and annual by submitting the best of their year's work, and also of course to the jury members who give up their valuable time to do the judging;

Simon Sharville for his creative impact and diplomacy during the design process;

Sabine Reimer who has co-ordinated the production with highly effective organisational skills and pragmatism;

Stella Di Meo who - with great imagination - has found and established the new venue, organised the exhibition and developed the marketing and communications strategy;

Brian Cronin for the use of his illustration 'Chinese Boy' on the cover;

Katharina Manolessou for the use of her illustration 'Monkeypants' on the Images 31 Call for Entries form;

Stuart Briers for his ongoing support (IT and anything else) and patience when faced with yet another question about the correct use of the AOI database;

All our dedicated casual staff and volunteers for their invaluable assistance with the competition and exhibition, in particular: Rebecca Fox, Emily Jepps, Chloe King, Chetan Kumar, Akiko Tamura and Toshiko Tanaka; and special thanks to Dorothee Dines who helped to implement our marketing and press strategy;

Last but not least, my colleagues from the AOI Images Committee who I have not mentioned yet, Stephanie Alexander and Adam Graff.

Finally, congratulations to all of this year's winners. Images represents the cream of illustration. Well done.

Russell Cobb
AOI Chairman

Professional identity

When the request came to contribute this introduction an image immediately entered my mind. It was that of the captain of a prestigious ocean liner being interviewed on the television news a few years back. Looking improbably like an ol' seadog from one of Joseph Conrad's novels he stood foursquare while the journalist rattled on and when handed the microphone immediately said, "You must be pretty short on news if you've come all this way to talk to me." The parallels between this sardonically pragmatic character being bothered by the news networks and myself being asked to write for the annual are not at all that close, of course, but I did wonder why the responsibility and distinction of being asked to contribute this piece was being extended to an historian.

Typically the introductions are the preserve of practitioners and commissioning agents and generally concerned with questions of gravity to the profession and I agonised over what the hell I could usefully contribute to the debate. Eventually I decided that the central focus of my past research and subsequent lectures was not only good enough for the piece but perhaps also timely. It is nothing less than the professional identity of the practising illustrator. I should explain.

Students attending my lectures hear me occasionally lament the lack of a positive cultural identity experienced among contemporary practising illustrators, no matter how successful and well-known, that leaves me both baffled and disappointed. I know, as an historian, that British illustrators are the inheritors of a rewarding, gutsy, past which should give a sense of satisfaction at its achievement and a pleasure at being 'in the line' today with the possibilities of contributing to that

history. There should be a proper sense of presence in the culture of British art and a proper sense of self-respect in the profession. But perhaps here is the first problem: is illustration a profession? Perhaps sociologists would question whether it was and be happier describing it as a loose association of like-minded practitioners without any binding codes of conduct that are found in the more readily identified professions such as the law and medicine. Well, the AOI has of course done much to create and promote codes of business, with varying success, but it is a fact that historically illustrators have been pretty resilient to the idea of becoming a formal band of brothers (and sisters) preferring apparently the highs and lows, risks and fortunes, of being freelancers.

When, for example, in the 1890s the London Sketch Club became the unofficial headquarters of professional illustrators in the metropolis it hosted a group of (almost exclusively, I believe) men in a bohemian bond of camaraderie that even then, with the reputation of many ensuring them the status of household names, was without legal or codified business practises underpinning it. I'm sure they saw no sense in it.

And yet their 'brotherhood' did provide them with a sense of achievement and gave a proper sense of value to themselves, the arts and society at large. 'Professionalism' to them wasn't to be found enshrined in any formal rigmarole but was encountered and preserved in the practises they were good at and proud of. Drawing for a living was for them a respectable business with the bonus of conferring on the individuals who practised it a relative freedom denied other workers.

illustration: Paul Slater

Leo De Freitas is an illustration historian with early research projects such as 'The decline of trade wood engraving in Britain 1880-1914' and modest little studies on the Victorian illustrators Charles Robinson and Arthur Rackham to his name. He also published a study of John Tenniel's illustrations to the two 'Alice' books, researched and successfully submitted a PhD thesis on the 'Early history of trade engraving in Britain 1700-1880'. Since 1986, he has eked out a livelihood as a lecturer and writer on illustration and as an exhibition organiser; his own personal venture, Graphicus Touring, creates and tours exhibitions of excellence in the graphics arts. To date Thomas Bewick, Thomas Rowlandson, John Tenniel, Geoff Grandfield, Dave McKean and Paul Slater have all been artists highlighted. From 1986 until 2004 he was the organiser of the Victoria and Albert's annual illustration awards. His latest published study (2004) is on the 'Banbury chapbooks' - examples of 18th & 19th century popular print culture - with a particular interest in their illustration.

In an essential way, this professional identity seems lacking today. Undoubtedly, the exigencies of 'doing business' in a modern international capitalist-consumerist culture, whilst bestowing benefits our Victorian and Edwardian forebears couldn't have dreamt of, are unsympathetic to such niceties as professional identity but I don't see why this necessarily prevents illustrators from forging and promoting their own unique (for that's what it would be) collective character.

"Yeah, and how would that be done?"

Of course I see the history of illustration playing an important role in this identity problem. Students know of my amnesia analogy. I ask them to imagine going to bed one night and suffering complete loss of memory. In the morning they would awake not knowing who they are, where they came from and what ambitions they had for themselves in the future. They'd survive but they would be seriously, if not completely, disorientated. I often find myself believing contemporary illustrators are in that position. Frequently not knowing the depth and the richness of their professional history and the cultural importance of illustration to the modern world (for me, by the way, that means from the 16th century onwards) means that they are without the scope of achievement and the sense of purpose necessary for the creation of a professional identity.

Their history would show, as it frequently does, that there is nothing new under the sun; work gets done and bills don't get paid (Thomas Bewick in the early 1800s pursued one bill owing him - by an ex apprentice - for decades), technological shift brings tears and opportunities (the new photo-technologies of the 1880s and 1890s both robbed some of a livelihood and yet expanded the horizon for a new illustration with opportunities for others), 'style' is a double edged sword (poor old Louis Wain couldn't make a penny unless he was drawing his - for us - infamous cats) and success breeds envy and deceit (Kate Greenaway may have been the first professional to suffer plagiarising of her work - with a pecuniary loss to herself of course). Such a history - and not the 'pictorial' one of the art historian, the bibliophile and the collector - gives a three-dimensionality to the past activity of professional illustration and is an enrichment of the experience which can feed into and help support the identity of today's practitioners. To know this history helps orientate the artist with the likelihood of stiffening a resolve to be pleased and confident about being an illustrator.

Wow! The sea captain I started with certainly did not go on a rant like the above - but then, he had a pride in his professional identity that was completely unshakeable.

From the wider perspective, I profit from, I see and hear history repeating itself in the art of contemporary professional illustration. The knee jerk journalism surrounding the advent of the Apple Mac and digitised image making (anyone else noticed how most negative reviews of the place of illustration in the post 1980s world of graphics was written by those with vested interests?) can find its less hyperbolical cousin in Victorian journalism describing the new invention of photography; the doomsters prophesying the death of print and print dependent illustration will be found, I suspect, in the trade magazines and popular press that announced the advent of public television, the video, the web - it's such an easy, immediate, bandwagon, piece of copy to write, isn't it! Illustrators and their art did not so much survive the assaults technological progress made upon them in the past as adapt and innovate to changing practises and new opportunities.

We have the same issues going on today. Whether working in a traditional manner and using the computer as a chunk of hardware with which to do business or widening aesthetic horizons through the exploitation of the new generations of software contemporary illustrators are engaging with the world of commerce and profit as they have always done and I cannot see any reason not to imagine the illustrative image being a continuing part of the rich diversity of pictorial experience we enjoy. Take a look inside, you'll see what I mean.

Dr Leo J De Freitas

'I love illustration. It is a particularly interesting period at the moment and has been increasingly so since I started. There seem to be more illustrators working commercially and with a broader range of styles than ever before. More importantly there also seems to be more attention given to illustration in magazines and books than ever before. Long may it continue . . .'

Daniel Moorey

Advertising

'… trends have come and gone but the premise of illustration has always remained the same: a single image can attract an audience in style alone, whilst enabling your creative mind to run wild.'

Derek Bain

Judges

Derek Bain
KLP Euro

Derek Bain has been working with illustrators on through-the-line accounts for over 12 years. In this time trends have come and gone but the premise of illustration has always remained the same: a single image can attract an audience in style alone, whilst enabling your creative mind to run wild. For those reasons he will always turn to illustration whenever briefs allow.

Greg Burne
Director, Big Active, Creative Management, London

Greg was educated in North Wales and completed his degree in Illustration at Liverpool Polytechnic. He is the director of the Illustration division of Big Active, the London based Creative Consultancy. He represents some of the world's leading illustrators. Big Active have produced work for many prominent brands, magazines and bands including, The Chemical Brothers, Nike, Adidas, Gucci, Coke and many others.

Mick Marston
Illustrator and Senior Lecturer in Graphic Design at Leeds Metropolitan University

Now hiding behind the banner of The Futile Vignette Company and approximately one third of Fine 'n' Dandy, he has been an illustrator for 10 years. In addition to this he lectures at Leeds Metropolitan University.

Daniel Moorey
Head of Art Buying, DDB London

Daniel studied anthropology and art but somehow ended up working in advertising. He has been an art buyer for the last ten years. Having started out at Abbott Mead Vickers he is now Head of Art Buying at DDB London.

Henry Obasi
Illustrator

Born in 1967, Henry Obasi studied Visual Communication at Central St.Martins, and came to the public's attention 4 years ago with an ad campaign for Firetrap clothing. His career has gone from strength to strength, illustrating and designing for a range of global clients from Nike, Sony Playstation, Nickelodeon, Kangol, Redbull, Vespa to name a few.

GOLD

Gary Embury

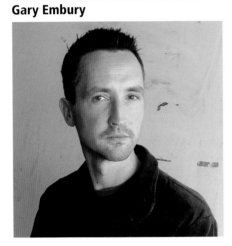

Micro Box

Medium	Mixed Media
Brief	One of a series of press ads comissioned for Microsoft illustrating lateral thinking outside the box.
Commissioned by	Jim Landen
Client	Barkers
Commissioned for	Microsoft

Gary Embury has been an illustrator for the last 20 years, during which time he has worked for a wide variety of advertising, editorial and publishing clients, including The Saturday Times supplement, Radio Times, The Economist, New Scientist, The Guardian, The Telegraph, Aardman Animation, Penguin Books, Barclays Bank, British Telecom, and the NSPCC. He has also exhibited his work in solo and group shows in London and Paris where he lived and worked.

He is a senior Lecturer in Illustration at The Arts Institute at Bournemouth and is currently completing an MA at Kingston University.

1   Early sketches
2   Client visual
3-5   Further sketches
6   Final illustration

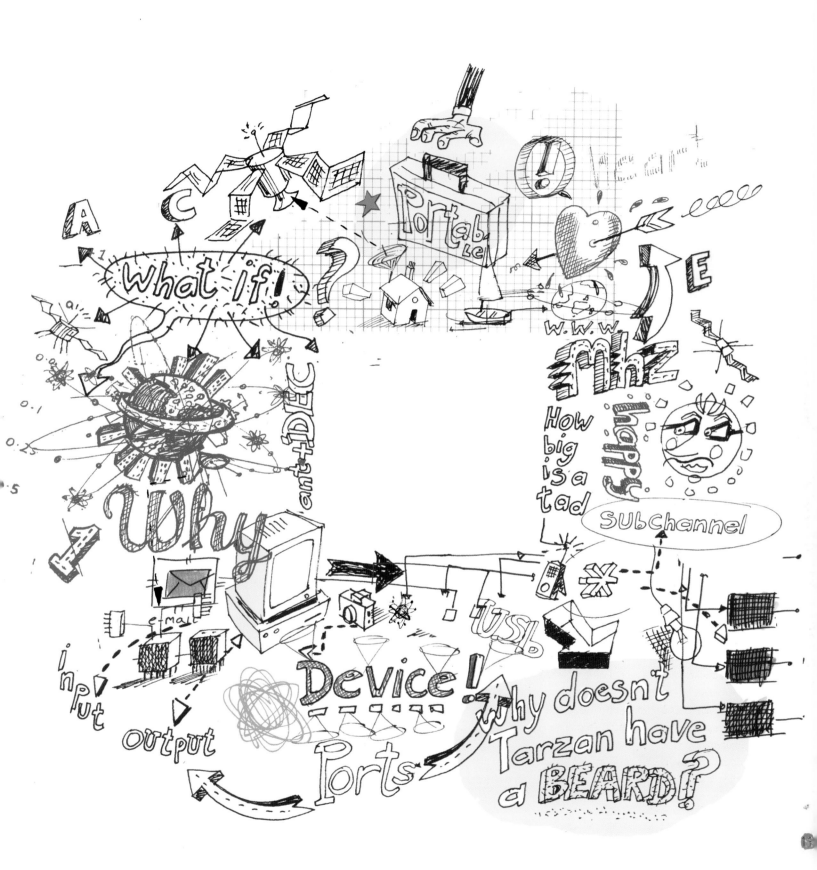

SILVER

Ben Weeks

Smoke Signal

Medium	Ballpoint pen, lined paper & digital
Brief	Open with corporate brand values as a guide: passion, vision & creativity.
Commissioned by	James Sommerville, Grant Dickson
Client	ATTIK
Commissioned for	Noise 5 Poster

Ben has a strong desire to contribute to the wellbeing of others and genuinely enjoys helping people. Although he tends to be a private, sensitive person and is not generally a visible leader, he nevertheless works quite intensely with those close to him, quietly exerting influence behind the scenes. He has great depth of personality, is complex himself and can understand and deal with complex issues and people.

His illustrations are recognized internationally by: The Art Director's Club of New York, American Illustration, Pizza Express Prospects, Juxtapoz, Applied Arts, Mac User, and Creativity.

In 2004, Ben graduated with a Master's Degree from ATTIK and the University of Huddersfield on a full scholarship. After, he worked freelance, then full time for ATTIK continuing his role in projects for Nike, Scion, Smith Barney, EA Games, Sobe, AOL and Siemens.

In late 2004, Ben returned to Toronto and launched his own studio and consultancy. Some of his clients include: Res Magazine, Soapbox Design Inc, Pen Canada, The Walrus Magazine and a Japanese company who recently bought the rights to reproduce this image for sale on t-shirts across Japan.

San Francisco's gone all Upper Class.

UPPER CLASS SUITE   Now on all flights to San Fran. *Book at virgin.com/atlantic*

virgin atlantic

BRONZE

Jonathan Williams

San Francisco's Gone All Upper Class

Medium	Photoshop
Brief	To create an image which promotes the Virgin Atlantic Upper Class suite by mixing cliches of the British landed gentry with familiar aspects of San Francisco.
Commissioned by	Alex Bamford
Client	Rainey Kelly Campbell Roalfe / Y&R
Commissioned for	Virgin Atlantic Airways

Graduating with a Masters Degree from Edinburgh College of Art in 1992, Jonathan Williams has worked in publishing as a designer and art director commissioning some of the UK's most celebrated artists including Tony Ross, Jan Pienkowski and Nick Sharratt. Inspired and excited by the illustrators he was working with, Jonathan turned freelance himself in 2000. His images now appear in major publications, books and retail outlets across Europe, America and Australia for prestigious clients such as Paramount, Time Warner, Benetton, Unilever and Virgin. His work has also featured in American Illustration, Graphik, Creative Match, Design Week and the AOI Images annual. Jonathan lives and works from a farmhouse in the Buchan plains north of Aberdeen, a beautiful and sometimes desolate setting best viewed from a fur-lined parka.

13

'Illustration right now is alive and
kicking, it is about collaboration,
mash-ups, self-initiated projects,
mixed media, call it what you will,
visual communication surrounds
us like never before.
The illustrators want a piece of the
action, and they are getting it!'

Paul Burgess

Books

'I thought the standard was
very high and the variety
of illustration very exciting.
It was a pleasure to be
able to look at so many
beautiful pieces of work.'

Louise Power

'Picture books are often our first introduction to the visual
and literary arts. As an art form with limitless possibilities,
they have long provided illustrators with an arena for
radical experimentation. That ripe arena is threatened
today by the tyranny of the international market and
pressure to create culturally neutral, rather than culturally
distinct, work'

Elizabeth Hammill

Paul Burgess

Illustrator, Senior Lecturer in Illustration at the University of Hertfordshire

Paul Burgess is a freelance Illustrator and Designer, working in publishing, editorial and music graphics. He is currently Senior Lecturer in Illustration at the University of Hertfordshire, and also teaches on the Illustration course at the University of Brighton. Paul is the co-author of the book 'Satellite: Sex Pistols Graphics, Photography and Fashion', published by Abstract Sounds in 1999, and has worked closely with the Sex Pistols on numerous occasions as a graphic designer.

Elizabeth Hammill

Artistic Director, Sevenstories, Newcastle

Elizabeth Hammill is a Founding Director of Sevenstories, the Centre for Children's Books, a literary project that she initiated and developed over ten years as Artistic Director. Currently working with illustrators and authors to establish the centre's collection, she brings her experience as a curator, children's bookseller, literary festival programmer, critic and university lecturer to all her work.

'Images speak louder than words, and today's illustrators are in fine voice.'

Sophie Stericker

Stefan Haupt

Production Manager, Tokyopop, Hamburg, Germany

After graduating in architecture, Stefan Haupt started working as a freelance graphic designer and musician in the 90s. Now he is Production Manager at Tokyopop and responsible for book cover layouts. Tokyopop is a specialist Manga publisher with headquarters in Tokyo and Los Angeles.

Louise Power

Freelance Art Consultant, London

Louise Power is a freelance Art Consultant primarily working with Walker Books. She is well-known for visiting art colleges around the UK giving talks about illustrating children's books, character development and what publishers look for when artwork is submitted. She has had many years experience in linking artists with publishers.

Sophie Stericker

Creative Director, HarperCollins Children's Books, London

Sophie Stericker has worked with illustration for the last 15 years. After graduating from Camberwell School of Art she worked for a small design consultancy and thereafter for HarperCollins Children's Books. She loves the challenges and diversity of the children's book market and gets great joy from working with some of the most talented and creative illustrators in the world. (I am most fortunate, I know!).

GOLD

Matthew Richardson

In Evil Hour

Medium	Mixed Media
Brief	Penguin cover illustration for 'In Evil Hour' by Gabriel Garcia Marquez. Almost a thriller - the story is set in the oppressive heat of a South American town, dominated by the catholic church.
Commissioned by	Jonathan Gray
Client	Gray 318
Commissioned for	Penguin

Matthew Richardson was born and brought up in London and studied BA Graphic Design at Middlesex Polytechnic followed by postgraduate study in illustration at Central St Martins. Inspiration for illustrative work at this time was sought in untamed, out-of-the-way, in-between places such as folk art, outsider environments, children's drawing and the work of artists such as Jean Dubuffet, Jiri Kolar, Marcel Duchamp and Susan Hiller.

He has worked for many and varied clients over the years including the London Sinfonietta, Carling, Channel 4 Television, Penguin Books, Hodder, The British Council, The Guardian, Quartet Books, The Sunday Times, New Scientist, World of Interiors, BT, Decca and EMI. He was commissioned by Addison to illustrate the 2004 Annual Report for WPP.

The gold award image is one of a series of cover illustrations for the books of Gabriel Garcia Marquez published by Penguin. Matthew's illustration for Marquez's 'Love In the Time of Cholera' won a bronze award in Images 29.

Alongside working to commission, Matthew also pursues and exhibits his own work which utilises a diverse range of processes such as print, photography, drawing, the moving image, assemblage and various digital media. In 2004, he gained an MA in Fine Art at UWIC, Cardiff and ideas explored on this course have since fed back into his illustration work. In 2005, Matthew's work was shown as part of the exhibition 'Beginning, Middle and End' at g39 in Cardiff.

Matthew currently teaches part-time on the BA Illustration course at Herefordshire College of Art and Design.

1   Early sketches
2   Published cover
3   Final illustration

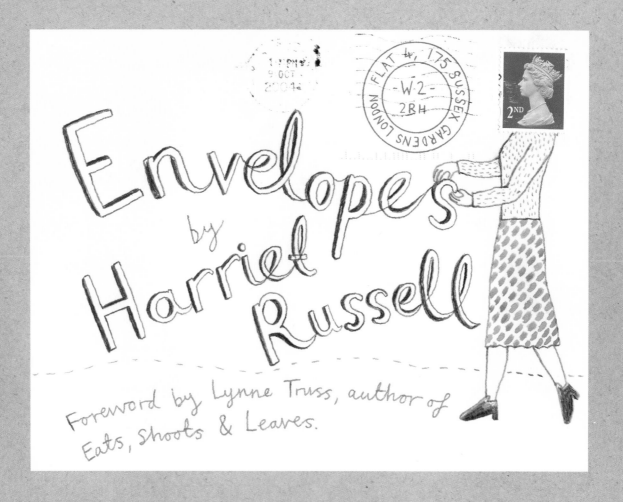

SILVER

Harriet Russell

Envelopes

Medium	**Mixed Media**
Brief	Cover for own book of decorated envelopes which have all been sent through the post and been addressed in a variety of different creative ways.
Commissioned by	**Robbin Schiff**
Client	**Random House, New York**
Commissioned for	**Random House**

Harriet Russell has been drawing all her life and wanted to be an illustrator ever since she wrote and illustrated one of her first stories at the age of 8. 'The Black Teeth' was about a family who steal and eat all their children's sweets whilst they are asleep. She has progressed a little since then, although her ideas are now even sillier. An alphabet where 'A is for rhinoceros' and 'K is for fish with an umbrella' being a good example.

Her book 'Envelopes' was published by Random House, New York in 2005. The book is a collection of 75 decorated envelopes created by Harriet, which are addressed in a large variety of different creative ways: mazes, join-the-dots, crossword puzzles, puns, visual games and literary wordplay. The majority of envelopes were delivered safely to their intended destinations and all have postmarks to prove it!

Harriet studied at Glasgow School of Art and Central Saint Martins where she completed her MA in 2001. She has worked for a number of clients including Penguin books, Simon and Schuster, 4 Creative, Christian Aid, Independent on Sunday, Hodder and Walker books.

BRONZE

Jonny Hannah

Mr. Satchelmouth

Medium	Mixed Media
Brief	To write & illustrate a homage to the greatest trumpeter who ever lived.
Commissioned by	Deirdre McDermott
Client	Walker Books

Jonny Hannah was born and bred in Dunfermline, in the kingdom of Fife.

He studied illustration at Liverpool Art School, where he was taught by the legendary Peter Bailey. Since he graduated from The Royal College of Art in 1998, he has constantly worked as an illustrator in most fields.

In 2000 he completed the collaboration with animator Jonathan Hodgson on 'The Man With The Beautiful Eyes', a five minute animation for Channel Four Television which went on to win umpteen awards, including a BAFTA in the same year.

Jonny likes to spend some of his hard earned money on his cottage industry, Cakes & Ale Press, screenprinting books, posters, prints and boxed sets. In 2001, he co-published 'The Captain's Alphabet' with Peter Sampson at Merivale Editions, which like most of his fine printed ephemera, quickly sold out.

'Hot Jazz Special', published by Walker Books, is a book of red-hot rhymes and cool cats, and his first offering for children. His other passions include Hank Williams and Emmett Miller at The Unquiet Grave.

He often wears correspondent shoes and enjoys the odd fine whisky whilst constantly pondering the life and times of the mysterious Rocket Man.

'At Northbank we see ten photographers for every good
illustrator but with the renaissance of the craft perhaps
this balance will change?

Robert Shaw

'I resent the fact that illustration is often perceived as
the poor relation of design and fine art. A number of
illustrators I admire, frustrated by constricting briefs, now
forge successful careers in the field of fine art.
For me the ubiquitous T-shirt acts as a canvas for much of
the illustration I enjoy, perhaps due to the freedom and
accessibility it offers to the artist.'

James Fairbank

Design & New Media

Lucinda Rogers

'With the advance into the digital world the possibilities for
image creation are endless and fascinating, yet ever more
important is the need to escape the screen, be inventive
and get our hands dirty!'

Lara Harwood

James Fairbank
Retail Manager, Carhartt, Newburg St.
His involvement in illustration first started with a number of chance friendships with people involved in illustration, for some reason he just seemed to gravitate towards them. Working with Carhartt furthered this interest as they prefer to use emerging artists so he was always on the look out for new, fresh work. An interest in Edo period Japanese illustration and its connection to contemporary tattooing also appeals to him and small BMX brands (especially Michael Sieben's work for TerribleOne) also provide constant inspiration.

Lara Harwood
Illustrator
After completing undergraduate studies in Graphics at Camberwell College of Art in 1989, Lara established a broad client base working as a freelance illustrator. Currently at the Chocolate Factory in North London, she combines her commissioned work with exhibitions of works on canvas and printmaking.

Helen Osborne
Agent, Heart, London
Helen studied Graphics at Camberwell College of Art and since graduating in 2001, has worked as a senior team member at Heart. Helen played a major role in the New York sister company's 4000sq ft launch exhibition at The Art Directors Club of America in November 2003 and continues to divide her time between the London and New York offices. She also co-edits and art directs the agency's BEAT publication.

John Rushworth
Partner, Pentagram, London
John Rushworth graduated in 1981 with a First Class Honours Degree in graphic design from Preston College of Art. He began his career with Michael Peters Ltd and then worked for Conran Design Group before joining Pentagram in 1983. In 1987 he became Pentagram's first associate and in 1989 he was invited to become a Partner. His work spans the development of major, strategically driven identities through to craft-based design programmes.
He has received many international awards including a gold medal at the Lahti Poster Biennale and D&AD silver awards for the Crafts Council, The Four Seasons Hotel, Polaroid, and The Berkeley Hotel. In 1995 John was elected a member of the Alliance Graphique Internationale and he is currently an external assessor at Falmouth College of Art and the University of Lancashire.

Robert Shaw
Creative Director, Northbank, London
He likes illustrators. He must do, he married one. Perhaps he was drawn by the lucrative commissions (London in the 80s was a good time to be able to draw), or was it simply that illustration can inspire and complement design? The sense of discovery of a new or emerging talent or the power of a memorable illustration can still stop him in his tracks. Those who can embrace change, bring value and energy to a brief or just have a playful view of the world will always add a layer of emotion to a design. Mind you, it still annoys him to find paint brushes where his toothbrush should be.

'I was impressed by the very skillfully executed entries and the degree of professionalism I saw. The quality of the entered work was exceptional and made the selection process very hard indeed.'

John Rushworth

21

GOLD

Orly Orbach

Burnt Book Box

Medium	Burn Marks and Ink on Laminated Paper, Burnt Wooden Box
Brief	An arts and health project which aims to raise awareness about issues related to smoking. As the girl smokes the burn marks spread through the pages.
Commissioned by	Lisa Shephard (Arts Development Officer)
Client	Cannock Chase Council
Commissioned for	Reality Check. Message in a Box

Orly Orbach' s approach to illustration has a strong focus on research, experimentation and play. Using deep tones to produce highly atmospheric images, her work contains personal narratives and communicates on an emotional level.

"When I'm drawing I access my emotional palette, and imagine being the character or experiencing the situation that I am illustrating. The work I produce is closer to theatre than to commercial art."

Her interest in theatre and performance has led to numerous collaborations with musicians and composers, actors and live-artists. Past commissions show the diversity of her practise, and include: 'Ghost Watch' – an installation for the Hayward Gallery, 'Adapting to Light' – a film made in collaboration with the composer Lena Langer, and 'Nomadics'- a collaborative multi-sensory installation at the Trinity Buoy Wharf.

As well as commissions, Orly Orbach contributes illustrations to publications such as Ambit and Le Gun. Her work has been exhibited widely, and her prints are in the Zebra gallery collection in Hampstead.

After studying Illustration at Brighton University and Communication Art and Design at the Royal College of Art, Orly Orbach became an artist-in-residence at Barnet college. She lives and works in London. Orly Orbach also facilitates workshops for schools and galleries, and is currently working as a creative consultant for Creative Partnerships.

1   Winning illustration
2-3 Published Box
4   Early sketches
5-6 Other illustrations

23

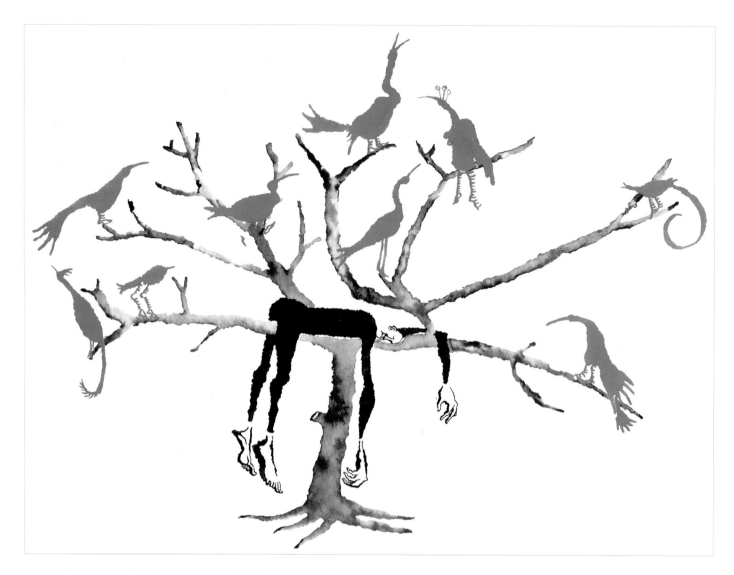

SILVER

Belle Mellor

Frames From 'Dawn Chorus'

Medium	Mixed Media
Brief	Produce a 30 second animated sting for MTV.
Commissioned by	Peter Moller/Jane Bolton
Client	MTV/Picasso Pictures
Commissioned for	MTV 'Artbreaks'

Belle graduated with a degree in Illustration from Bath Spa University College in 1994. She has worked extensively as a freelance illustrator for clients in the UK and further afield ever since. Her most prolific area to date has been the editorial field, enjoying the speedy deadlines and idea generation, but has also worked widely in advertising, design and publishing. Recent clients have included The Guardian, The Independent, The New York Times, The Economist, Shakespeare's Globe, The Wall Street Journal, CDP Travis Sulley and DMB&B.

With a growing enthusiasm for movement and sequential thinking, she undertook an MA in Animation at the RCA in 2003, whilst continuing with her commercial illustration practice.

Graduating in 2005, Belle had made 2 student films: "High" 2004 and "Sleep with the Fishes" 2005 plus a sting commissioned for MTV 'Artbreaks': "Dawn Chorus". They are currently being screened and entered into various international animation festivals, with the support of the British Council. 'Sleep with the Fishes' has recently won an international film prize and been shortlisted for the British Animation Awards. The films can be viewed on her website www.bellemellor.com

She has guest lectured at Goldsmiths, Bath Spa University College and Exeter School of Art & Design.

Belle lives and worries in Hove, continuing to produce illustration and animation.

BRONZE

Chris Watson

Lester Young

Medium	Mixed Media
Brief	Portrait of Lester Young for CD cover of classic Savoy jazz recordings.
Commissioned by	Carl Rush
Client	Crush design
Commissioned for	Savoy Jazz, Union Square Music Ltd.

Chris Watson works as an illustrator in publishing, music and fashion.

He completed a degree in Drawing and Painting at Glasgow School of Art, bucking the trend for white cube art with a riot of colour and content. Next he founded a collective to publish comic books and hold an exhibition in Glasgow. This led to Brighton where he graduated from MA Sequential Design and Illustration in 2002.

In 2003, Chris exhibited Bad Motorcycle a series of screen prints in a decorated box at Tatty Devine and Cinch in London and launched his own limited edition t-shirt label, Ton-Up Press. Chris is a devotee of underground culture and a keen motorcyclist. The label is named for the Ton-Up kids, the first UK street cult to create their own status from customised clothing & machines.

Screen prints and t-shirts have been featured in Creative Review, Wallpaper, Time Out, Face, FHM and snapped up from boutiques like Colette in Paris, Arcuate in Tokyo & www.TonUpPress.com Recently he's designed images and type for labels like LaRocka, Loaded and Levi's.

Chris also works in editorial where he enjoys the constant challenge of doing something fresh often with tight deadlines and dry texts. Clients include the Guardian Guide, Media Guardian, BBC Online, The Idler, British Council, RD Living & Management Today.

Lester Young is from a series of 13 Jazz CD covers. It came about from the client seeing a portrait of Babs Gonzales, a piece of personal work printed in Straight No Chaser magazine.

'The role of the Illustrator has
become more credible as the barriers
between the disciplines fall. I feel
this is no coincidence.'

Adrian Johnson

Editorial

'I'm so pleased that illustrators are getting out
their pencils and drawing again.
Photoshop should always be used as a means to
an end; there's nothing worse than and illustration
that relies on flashy effects in Photoshop.'

Anamaria Stanley

Roanne Bell
DVD Editor/Freelance Design Writer,
Creative Review, London
She left Creative Review magazine, where she was editor
of the reviews and design sections and the bi-annual
DVD, in August 2003 after four-and-a-half happy years.
While she continues to produce the magazine's DVD,
her other clients include Pentagram Design, British
Television Advertising Awards and Iranian design
magazine, Neshan. Roanne has co-edited two books on
contemporary illustration with Pentagram partner Angus
Hyland: Pen and Mouse (2001) and Hand to Eye (2003),
both published by Laurence King Publishing.
A third LKP book, Pictures and Words: New Comic Art
and Narrative Illustration, co-edited with Creative Review
senior writer Mark Sinclair, launched in Autumn 2005.

Paul Davis
Image-Maker
Born in Somerset, England 1962.
Moved to London in 1985 and has been there ever since.
Apparently, he is an image-maker of our confused and
restless times.

Adrian Johnson
Illustrator
Adrian Johnson has worked prolifically in illustration
for the last 9 years across editorial, advertising, and
children's book fields picking up various awards both in
the UK and abroad. He is a founding and core member
of Black Convoy and teaches part-time at Kingston
University.

Stuart Selner
Creative Director, Marie Claire Magazine, London
Stuart Selner has commissioned illustrations right across
the board from prestigious fashion magazines to youth
titles and lad mags. He is now in his fifth year as Creative
Director of Marie Claire. Previous positions include being
Creative Director of Arena and Elle and of the youth
portfolio at Emap Elan. He also spent time in New York
where he oversaw the launch of FHM America and was
Associate Art Director on Seventeen.

Anamaria Stanley
Studio Manager, Time Out Magazine, London
Anamaria Stanley has commissioned illustrations for
more years than she cares to remember and most of
those years have passed by at Time Out. She considers
herself lucky in that she had been given the opportunity
to work across a wide spectrum of subject matter and
style. She feels it has granted her a unique view.

GOLD

Paul Blow

Mother

Medium	Digital
Brief	To illustrate the article "How I Broke Up With My Mother".
Commissioned by	Bruno Howard
Client	The Guardian
Commissioned for	The Guardian Weekend Magazine

Paul Blow was born in Falkirk, Scotland in 1969. A year later, he and his family moved to Brighton finally settling in Dorset. In 1992, he graduated from Maidstone College of Art and immediately began working as a professional illustrator. He continued his studies at Brighton University and in 1994, graduated with an MA in Illustration.

Paul works for both UK and US clients and exhibits his paintings and digital prints regularly in London, New York and Dorset.

Aside from his gallery shows and illustration work, Paul also devotes a portion of his time lecturing and teaching at the Arts Institute Bournemouth.

1   Visual
2   Final drawing
3   Final article
4   Winning illustration

LIVING WITHOUT MOTHER

When Kat Blackman received a hate-filled letter from her mother she broke all ties with her. Fourteen years on, it's a decision she's still glad she made …

I stopped communicating with my mother 14 years ago. I'd moved cities and she'd been to stay at my new house, and when she got back home she wrote me a vicious letter listing all the things she hated about my life: my job was "pretentious", my boyfriend was "dull", my house was "filthy". The first two points I could live with – the woman is entitled to her opinion – but my mother had given me a hygiene obsession and, as she was coming to stay, the house was far from filthy.

The letter rambled on about all sorts of disappointments I'd caused her and ended with this line: I wish you had never been born.

So the decision to cut her out of my life was easy. I never wrote back. I never phoned her again. And the only time she communicated with me after this was to send another hate-filled letter a year later when she'd heard about my new job. I didn't write back then, either. It would have been easier for me to put my feelings down on paper – to write a diatribe about her years of emotional and physical abuse. To accuse her of suffering from some personality disorder for which she should seek treatment. To purge my sadness, confusion and anger at her. To ask her why she let her bully of a boyfriend take out his hatred of children on my brother and me for so many years. I didn't because that would be to give her the attention she so desperately craved. Also, I didn't like her. Or, for that matter, love her.

Not having my mother in my life was cathartic. I enjoyed my new "mother-free" life and the eczema that had plagued my hands throughout my teenage years cleared up. I began to heal with the help of some close friends and a few self-help books. All the frightening, nasty and hateful things I'd suffered as a child became memories I chose not to revisit, and when I did I could put them into perspective and be philosophical about them making me into the person I am today.

Luckily I saw the potential to love via some amazing relationships, and two years ago I gave birth to my own daughter. I can't suppress my love for this child, and it gets stronger every day. Which is why, when people ask if I'll make contact with my mother again so she can meet her only grandchild, I say no. Never. She doesn't deserve to have us in her life and I could never explain to her what it is to love someone so much that you want to protect them from nasty people – because she never experienced maternal love herself.

The effect my non-relationship with my mother has had on my adult relationships is an ongoing distrust of other people's perfectly lovely mothers. But it hasn't affected my ability to keep a partner or make new friends, and I've always had a strong relationship with my very chilled-out father. He has never said anything judgmental to me about my attitude to his ex-wife.

It can be tricky explaining my situation to people who don't know what it is to be unwanted, and I'm jealous of them, really. People often think my situation is sad, when really it's the best possible outcome for me. I get so much love from my friends and my own little family that there is no gaping emotional hole in my life, and that's about as good a scenario as anyone could hope for.

Kat Blackman is a pseudonym

SHE DOESN'T DESERVE TO HAVE US IN HER LIFE

relationshipsspirit

The Guardian Weekend | May 21 2005 **75**

SILVER

David Hughes

Hilary Mantel

Medium	Mixed Media
Brief	Book review illustration for novelist Hilary Mantel's latest novel, 'Beyond Black'.
Commissioned by	Owen Phillips
Client	The New Yorker

David Hughes is a former postman who has been cursed with the dubious talent for drawing. It keeps him off the streets and out of the public library. David says that the only reason he got off his arse and submitted two illustrations to Images was the fact that he moved house this year and maybe to remind those that might actually pay to have illustration decorate their products, that Hughes is still alive and living in the UK.

The Hilary Mantel piece is one of those rare occasions that he was allowed a free hand and didn't suffer too much from interference from the art editor (Owen Phillips). There were some skulls in the original version, but Owen made Hughes delete the skulls.

The main reason Hughes works for US clients is that they pay better, but that's not saying much. He reckons the fees he got in the late 80's, early 90's were sometimes three times as much as the equivalent today.

He has just completed defacing Victor Hugo's classic 'The Hunchback Of Notre Dame' with approximately 140 illustrations: Translated/adapted by Jan Needle and to be published by Walker Books in November 2006. He feels it has revitalized and refreshed his enthusiasm for the genre. It is not a children's book. "Hats off to Walker Books" he says "for being brave enough to attempt the project".

Hughes is currently fulfilling commissions for Playboy Magazine, Esquire and Outside Magazine.

As Mr Bowden, David's coalman, says: "Mustn't grumble. You just got to keep on plodding on."

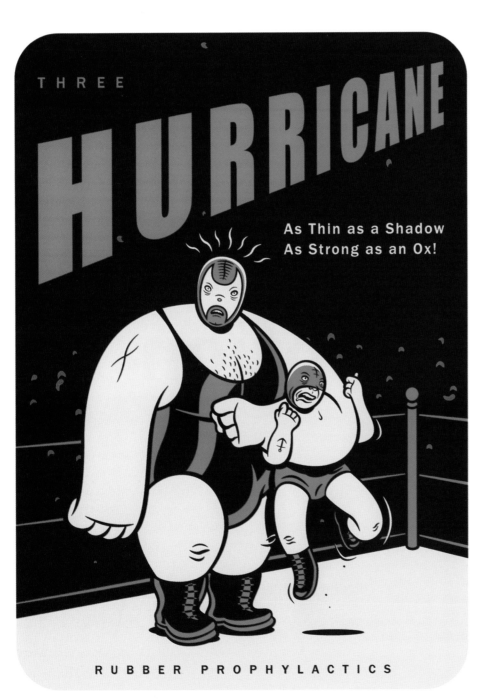

BRONZE

Nishant Choksi

Hurricane

Medium	Digital
Brief	Open brief - produced for Imbroglio Magazine, on the theme of painting, drawing and writing by artists.
Commissioned by	Rachel Thomson
Client	Imbroglio
Commissioned for	Imbroglio Magazine

Born in London and a graduate of Central St. Martins, Nishant entered the world of illustration in 2001. Influenced by the love of old Warner Bros. cartoons and the macabre wit of New Yorker cartoonists, such as Charles Addams, Nishant strives to create illustrations that look as though they already come with a history. His central pursuits are humorous characters, a delicate line and colours from an early printers palette.

Nishant has worked for a range of clients in the UK and abroad in advertising, book publishing and editorial fields.

Recent clients include: The Independent, The Wall Street Journal, Men's Health, Esquire New York, Transworld Publishers and Dyson.

31

'Illustration seems to me to be
going through a generally healthy
phase at the moment, although
I'd love to see more personal
and idiosyncratic thinking. This is
probably because I enjoy the luxury
of being asked to write and draw
my own material.'

Steven Appleby

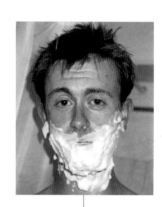

Jon Barraclough

Self Promotion

'I believe the standard of illustration is very high and
the breadth of talent impressive. This means that
commissioners are spoilt for choice.'

Christine Saunders

Judges

Steven Appleby

Steven Appleby's drawings have appeared in many newspapers in the UK and around the world. His other works as writer/artist include an animated television series, a BBC Radio 4 comedy series and over 15 books. He has also had numerous one-man exhibitions of paintings, prints and ceramics.

Jenny Cogliantry
Creative Director, 3+Co, New York

Jenny is a keen follower (and lover) of illustration. Her 12 years as a designer and art director have often allowed her to utilize the talents of illustrators from both the States (where she lives) and abroad. For her it is always an inspiring collaboration! She believes that this is an exciting time for illustration, with exceptional work being created across a vast array of mediums, for an ever-growing number of industries and audiences that have awakened to the power and value of illustrated content.

Nick Dewar
Illustrator

Nick Dewar was born in Scotland. He grew up in a small fishing town on the East Coast and attended Art School in Glasgow. Since then he has lived in Prague, London, New York and on a sheep farm in Cumbria. His work has appeared in magazines, on billboards, in books and on the wall next to the telephone. Illustration has been his sole occupation since leaving art school over 10 years ago and indeed it is doubtful that he could actually hold down a proper job if asked.

Christine Saunders
Life Coach of Photographers and Illustrators, Pathfinder, London

Christine has been involved with illustration for over 20 years. Most of that has been as an art buyer at agencies like DDB, JWT and Saatchi & Saatchi, but she has also spent a couple of years as an illustrators' agent. Nowadays she offers specialized career coaching for photographers and illustrators.

Lucie Stericker
Creative Director, Orion Group Publishing, London

As the Creative Director of Orion Books Lucie oversees all jackets and covers (hardback and paperback) dealing with many different creatives. She has been working in publishing for fifteen years.

'This year's standard of illustration is varied, from very talented to lamentable.'
Lucie Stericker

GOLD

Serge Seidlitz

USA Roadmap

Medium	Mixed Media
Brief	An illustrated map of America showing all 52 states and details about the US, for general portfolio and self promotion.

An English/ German hybrid, born in Kenya in 1977, Serge grew up traveling between the UK and Asia with his foreign correspondent father, where his exposure to modern Chinese art, Mad magazine and a constant diet of MTV, fuelled his desire to become an illustrator.

He spent some time at art school in London, and then as a designer at The Cartoon Network.

Serge currently lives and works in London and has an ever-evolving list of clients including MTV, VH1, Honda, Volvic, Orange, JWT, John Brown Citrus Publishing, The Guardian, the NME and Scarlett.

This sketch shows a different version of the concept. For the final drawing I decided to evolve the idea of the roads running through each state to link them altogether as it emphasized the idea of a road-trip.

SILVER

Paul Bommer

Night Vision

Medium	Digital
Brief	A personal meditation on night, light and sight.

Paul Bommer was born in Wembley into a large Polish/Welsh family, a few short months before the student uprisings broke out on the streets of Paris – although, to date, no clear link between the two events has been established.

He currently resides in the heart of the East End where he's been working as a freelance illustrator since late 2002.

In that time he has successfully built up a broad base of regular clients, including the Independent, the Financial Times and the Guardian.

Paul picked up his first pencil before he could walk and hasn't stopped scribbling since. He can often be seen crossing town weighed down by an enormous notebook, topping up his caffeine levels in one of London's many coffee houses and capturing the faces of characters walking by.

He always strives to create a unique and individual response to every commission. His work is marked by a strong graphic sense of invention, wit with an undercurrent of irreverence, and a love of character and wordplay.

He has been short listed twice for the SAA Transport for London poster competition and had work accepted into Images 27, 28, 29 and now, of course, Images 30.

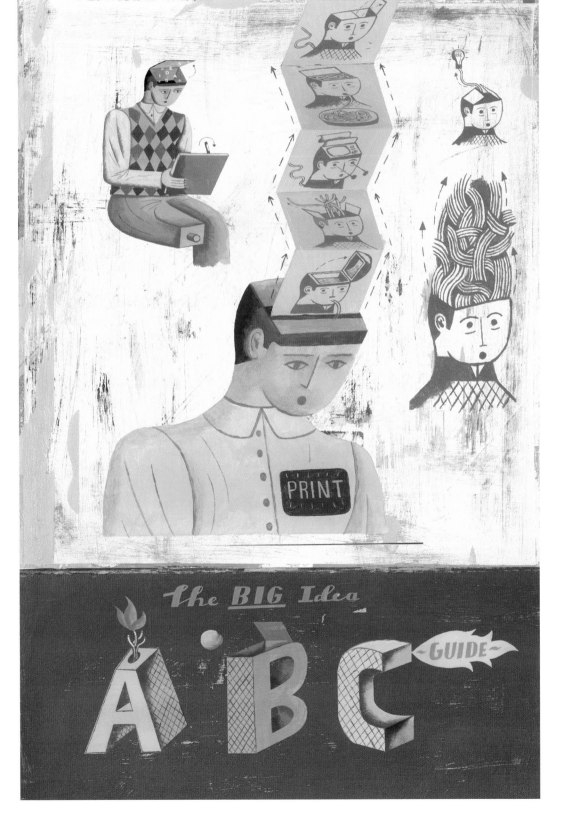

BRONZE

Russell Cobb

The ABC Guide To The Big Idea Volume 1

Medium	Acrylic
Brief	Cover image for a self promotion booklet about how to develop and obtain the big idea.

Russell is a graduate of Central St. Martin's School of Art. He graduated with an MA in 1997, receiving a distinction in communication design, illustration.

Russell's work has been widely published and has received many awards, including a D&AD Silver and 5 AOI Gold awards. He was also chosen as one of the Independent on Sunday's 'Top Ten Illustrators in the UK' in 2003. In 2004, Russell had a feature devoted to him in New York's prestigious 3x3 magazine, and in 2005 was voted by his peers as Chairman of the Association of Illustrators UK. Russell has also recently become a honorary member of the Society of Illustrators New York.

His working practise is based on hundreds of sketchbooks and working drawings, containing Russell's unique and quirky view of the world, and it's this working method that underpins his commissioned work.

"Not unlike Thurber's Walter Mitty, Russell Cobb lives his artistic life in a landscape created in his imagination."

37

The Collector by Kenneth Andersson

Selected by **Mark Reddy**

'I have lived with all the illustrations for a few weeks. I keep returning to this simply rendered, black and red brushed profile. It is simply the image that I most remember. In a world consumed by technical prowess I find the simple, visceral connection between hand, eye and paper to be the most compelling.'

**Mark Reddy, Head of Art,
Bartle Bogle Hegarty**

Mark Reddy is a visual itinerant. He has illustrated, designed, art directed, sculpted, gardened and generally made stuff all his life. But has never fallen out of love with commissioning all manner of imagery. Attempting to find space for artists and photographers to enable them to have fun in a world which seems to want to tell them how to do it. He has recently joined Bartle Bogle Hegarty as Head of Art.

Kenneth Andersson is an illustrator based in Sweden, where he lives with his family on an island outside Stockholm.
He works with art directors on print media, advertising agencies and book publishers.
He has also written and illustrated several children's books, some of them in co-operation with other writers.
His client list includes, amongst others, The Guardian, The Sunday Times Magazine, Newsweek, Daily News Magazine, Blender Magazine, Random House, Shots Magazine, BBC Radio Times.
Kenneth Andersson likes to play around with lines, bold or thin, straight or whacky, pen and brush, and likes to mix them up in the computer. Sometimes he adds some lines in the computer, too – there are some good lines in there.
Personal projects, exhibitions or various book projects – Andersson loves books! – often inspire his commissions.

The Collector

Images 30

Katherina Manolessou
Monkeypants

Editorial

Medium	Silkscreen Print
Brief	An illustration to accompany a weekly humourous agony aunt column which deals with love and sex problems in Athens.
Commissioned by	Stavroula Panagiotaki
Client	Athens Voice

Sarah Coleman

Great Britain

Self-Promotion

Medium	Mixed Media
Brief	Inspired by the words of Scor-zay-zee's* record, 'Great Britain' evolved into a 12x8ft exhibition piece celebrating our 21st century colours. *Google him!

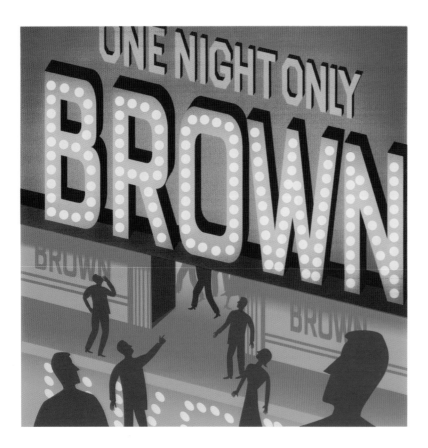

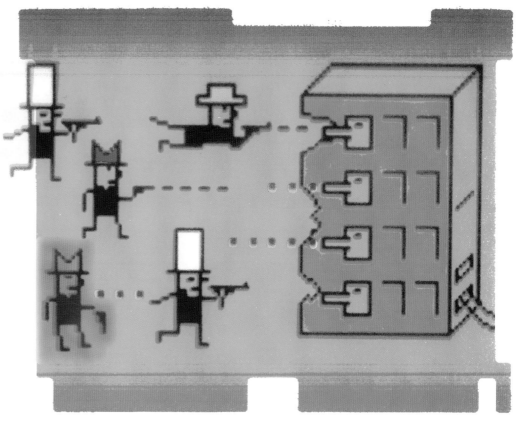

Andrew Baker
One Night Only: Arnold Brown

Editorial

Medium	Mixed Media
Brief	One night only: Arnold Brown. Comedian Arnold Brown talks on Radio 4 about the nature of... Brown.
Commissioned by	Jamie Trendall
Client	BBC Worldwide Ltd
Commissioned for	Radio Times

Andrew Baker
Black Hats And White Hats

Editorial

Medium	Mixed Media
Brief	Black hats and white hats attack a search engine. "The search engines will probably win but in the meantime it's a guerilla insurgency."
Commissioned by	Craig Mackie
Client	Reed Business Information Ltd
Commissioned for	New Scientist

Matthew Richardson
Alpha To Omega

Editorial

Medium	Digital
Brief	To create a wrap around cover to represent 'Alpha to Omega' for a New Scientist supplement on Cosmology
Commissioned by	Alison Lawn
Client	New Scientist

Matthew Richardson
Dark Matter

Editorial

Medium	Mixed Media
Brief	To Illustrate the concepts 'Black Holes and Dark Matter' for a feature on Cosmology.
Commissioned by	Alison Lawn
Client	New Scientist

Matthew Richardson
Leap To The Future

Design

Medium	Mixed Media
Brief	Cover illustration for 2004 annual report for WPP themed around animals and their traits.
Commissioned by	Feona McEwan/Rob Lamb/Guy Jefferson
Client	WPP/Addison
Commissioned for	WPP

Matthew Richardson

Mining The Imagination

Design

Medium	Mixed Media
Brief	Illustration for essay by Jeremy Bullmore on mining the imagination. Included in 2004 annual report for WPP themed around animals and their traits.
Commissioned by	Feona McEwan/Rob Lamb/Guy Jefferson
Client	WPP/Addison
Commissioned for	WPP

 Simon Pemberton
Sherlock, Billy And Me

Editorial

Medium	Mixed Media
Brief	Illustrate article discussing Sherlock Holmes's relationships with women and secret love affair with a foreign agent.
Commissioned by	Roger Browning
Client	The Guardian Newspaper
Commissioned for	The Guardian Review Cover

 Simon Pemberton
Bear & Bull

Editorial

Medium	Mixed Media
Brief	Demonstrate the phenomenon of 'bear' and 'bull' financial markets where only one can dominate at any one time.
Client	Worldwide Communications
Commissioned for	1930 Magazine

Simon Pemberton
Metamorphosis

Books

Medium	Mixed Media
Brief	Illustrate Franz Kafka's tale of an ordinary man who wakes up one morning transformed into an insect.
Commissioned by	Jamie Keenan
Client	Keenan Design
Commissioned for	Penguin Classics

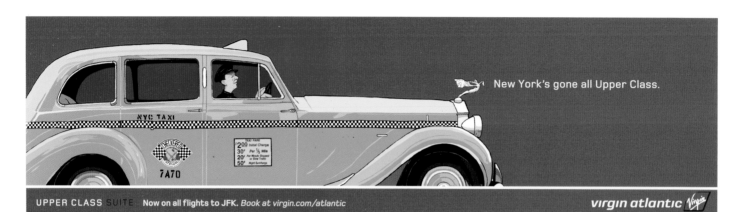

	Jonathan Williams			**Jonathan Williams**			**Jonathan Williams**
	New York's Gone All Upper Class			New York's Gone All Upper Class			Hong Kong's Gone All Upper Class
	Advertising			**Advertising**			**Advertising**
Medium	Photoshop		Medium	Photoshop		Medium	Photoshop
Brief	To create an image which promotes Virgin Atlantic's Upper Class Suite by mixing cliches of British landed gentry with familiar aspects of New York.		Brief	To create an image which promotes Virgin Atlantic's Upper Class Suite by mixing cliches of British landed gentry with familiar aspects of New York.		Brief	To create an image which promotes Virgin Atlantic's Upper Class Suite by mixing cliches of British landed gentry with familiar aspects of Hong Kong.
Commissioned by	Alex Bamford		Commissioned by	Alex Bamford		Commissioned by	Alex Bamford
Client	Rainey Kelly Campbell Roalfe / Y&R		Client	Rainey Kelly Campbell Roalfe / Y&R		Client	Rainey Kelly Campbell Roalfe / Y&R
Commissioned for	Virgin Atlantic Airways		Commissioned for	Virgin Atlantic Airways		Commissioned for	Virgin Atlantic Airways

Jonathan Williams
The Ragged Trousered Philanthropists

Books

Medium	Photoshop
Brief	To create a cover image for 'The Ragged Trousersed Philanthropists', the story of a group of painters and decorators oppressed by a capitalist system.
Commissioned by	Jim Stoddart
Client	Penguin
Commissioned for	Penguin Modern Classics

Jonathan Williams
San Francisco's Gone All Upper Class

Self-Promotion

| Medium | Photoshop |
| Brief | To create an image which mixes cliches of British landed gentry with familiar aspects of San Fransciso |

Jonathan Williams
Don't Believe The Lies

Editorial

Medium	Photoshop
Brief	To illustrate a feature about sensational (and fabricated) celebrity gossip.
Commissioned by	Silke Frohmann
Client	Condé Nast
Commissioned for	GQ (Germany)

 Spiral Studio
Human Traces

Editorial

Medium	Mixed Media
Brief	Illustration for an article on Sebastian Faulks's book "Human Traces". To encapsulate the general elements of the story.
Client	Waterstones
Commissioned for	Waterstones Magazine

 Spiral Studio
Romantic Adventures

Self-Promotion

Medium	Mixed Media
Brief	02 in a series of personal images dealing with the muse.

Philip Wrigglesworth

Brain Boosting

Editorial

Medium	Mixed Media
Brief	I was commissioned to create a striking, iconic image that encapsulated the idea of brain boosting, to be used as their front cover image.
Commissioned by	Craig Mackie
Client	New Scientist/RBI
Commissioned for	New Scientist

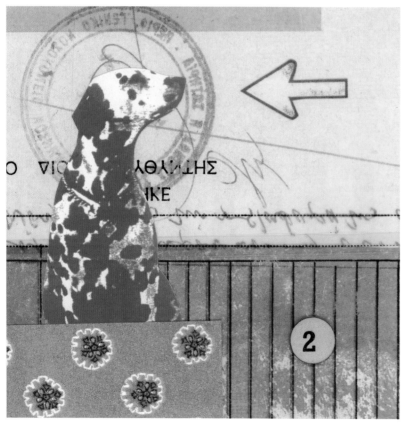

Jackie Parsons
Untitled

Self-Promotion

Medium   Mixed Media

Jackie Parsons
Untitled

Self-Promotion

Medium   Mixed Media

Carolyn Gowdy
Waiting For Mr Right

Editorial

Medium	Mixed Media
Brief	To illustrate a short story written at time of the Kimberley Fortier and David Blunkett scandal. Fictional, finely veiled, it is about the downfall of a pair of clandestine lovers.
Client	The Spectator Magazine
Commissioned for	Short Story in The Spectator Magazine

Mel Croft
Grey Pride

Editorial

Medium	Mixed Media
Brief	Illustrating an article about a retirement complex in Holland that caters for 'new age' and artistic people.
Commissioned by	Andrew Lee
Client	Financial Times
Commissioned for	FT Magazine

Lasse Skarbovik		**Lasse Skarbovik**		**Lasse Skarbovik**
Houses		Cookie		Bloomberg
Advertising		**Editorial**		**Editorial**

Medium	Digital		Medium	Digital		Medium	Digital
Brief	Cover for a brochure with information about the prizes and how to advertise in the magazine. The magazine is about and for house owners in Sweden.		Brief	"The way the cookie crumbles". How kid's food get to the mark.		Brief	Trust adminstration " Trustees can now cultivate better conditions for beneficaries, but they can also wind up in a thorny mess".
			Commissioned by	Jackie Shipley		Client	Bloomberg Wealth
Commissioned by	Cia Kilander		Client	Today's Parent Magazine			
Client	Fastighets Tidningen						

Lasse Skarbovik

Gourmet

Editorial

Medium	Digital
Brief	"Flying wine makers". Experts who help wine farmers around the world making the perfect wine.
Commissioned by	Cina Stegfors
Client	Gourmet Magazine

Lasse Skarbovik

Border

Self-Promotion

Medium	Digital
Brief	Self promotion. Illustration for an exhibition with the theme "Christmas in Europa"

Ian Whadcock
How To Trade Currencies

Editorial

Medium	Digital
Brief	Forex markets explained. The battle for supremacy in foreign exchange markets between the four key currencies: Dollar, Yen, Pound and Euro.
Commissioned by	Erica Morgan
Client	FT Business
Commissioned for	Investors Chronicle

Ian Whadcock
21st Century Supply Chain

Editorial

Medium	Digital
Brief	To illustrate an article about how Japanese automakers use a six-step supply chain system to build deeper supplier relationships with North American manufacturers.
Commissioned by	Kaajal Asher
Client	Harvard Business
Commissioned for	Harvard Business Review

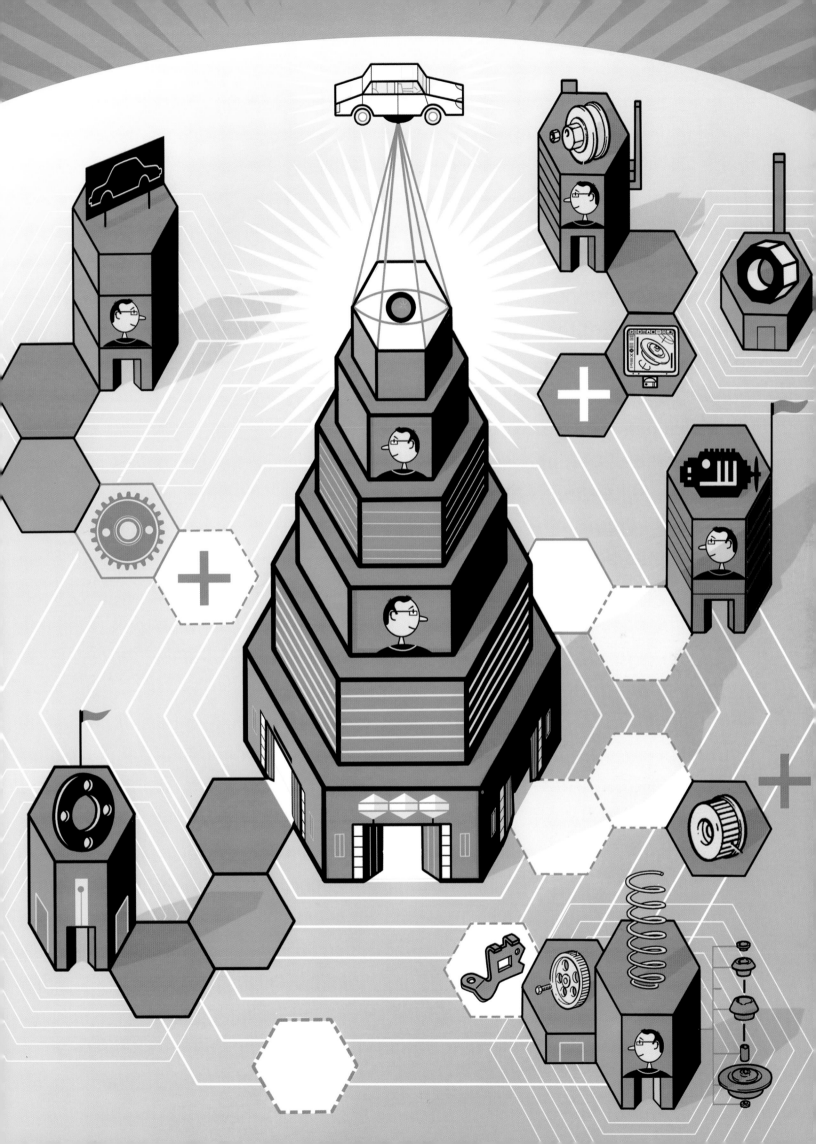

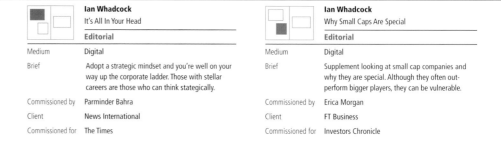

	Ian Whadcock			**Ian Whadcock**
	It's All In Your Head			Why Small Caps Are Special
	Editorial			**Editorial**
Medium	Digital		Medium	Digital
Brief	Adopt a strategic mindset and you're well on your way up the corporate ladder. Those with stellar careers are those who can think stategically.		Brief	Supplement looking at small cap companies and why they are special. Although they often out-perform bigger players, they can be vulnerable.
Commissioned by	Parminder Bahra		Commissioned by	Erica Morgan
Client	News International		Client	FT Business
Commissioned for	The Times		Commissioned for	Investors Chronicle

Andy Hammond
Cracker

Self-Promotion

Medium | Mixed Media

Brief | To come up with yet another christmas card that won't offend grandma too much.

Maria Raymondsdotter
Getting Old Is Funky

Editorial

Medium	Mixed Media
Brief	The new generation of pensioners has more money and an interest in fashion & travel.
Commissioned by	Mia Lifsten
Client	Åkesson & Curry
Commissioned for	Lust Magazine

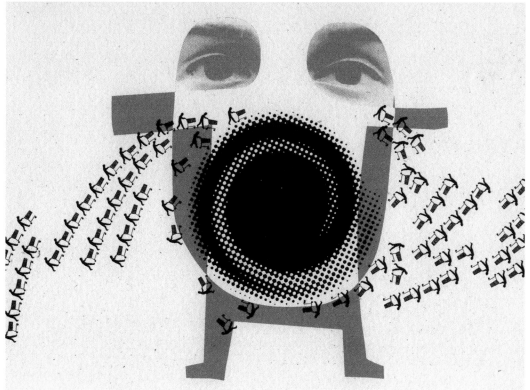

 Dettmer Otto
Orpheus

Self-Promotion

Medium | Digital

Brief | Mythology: Ovid's 'Metamorphoses'. Orpheus is granted his wish to lead his wife out of the underworld, on condition that he doesn't look back.

 Dettmer Otto
Hunger

Self-Promotion

Medium | Digital

Brief | Mythology: Ovid's 'Metamorphoses'. As punishment Erysichthon is infected by insatiable hunger.

Ian Dodds
The Loss

Editorial

Medium	Digital
Brief	This complex and deep story follows Mr Silverman through cities, characters and Dante's ninth circle of hell where he is confronted by his own insignificance.
Commissioned by	Sarah Morley
Client	The Independent on Sunday

Ian Dodds
Hope Denied

Editorial

Medium	Digital
Brief	A response to a true story of a Russian Human Rights campaigner and her plight for asylum after her son's kidnapping by the Russian Secret Service.
Commissioned by	Andrew Lee
Client	Financial Times Magazine

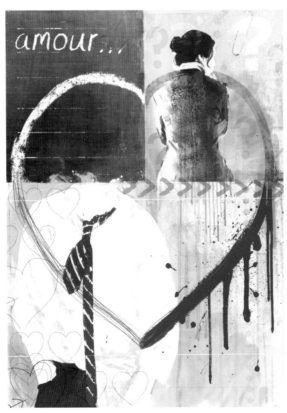

Ian Dodds
The Collector

Editorial

Medium	Digital
Brief	Collectors may be portrayed as sociopaths who prefer things to people but where would art be without Getty and Guggenheim?
Commissioned by	Andrew Lee
Client	Financial Times Magazine

Ian Dodds
Surviving The Sword

Editorial

Medium	Digital
Brief	In response to a book review, which recounts the Japanese treatment of POW told through diaries of some of the prisoners.
Commissioned by	Andrew Lee
Client	Financial Times Magazine

Ian Dodds
Teacher's Pet

Editorial

Medium	Digital
Brief	School Master Peter bumps into his old French teacher. It becomes clear that they share a secret and there may be some surprising lessons to be learned.
Commissioned by	Jamie Trendall
Client	Radio Times

Andy Potts
Lost N Found

Self-Promotion

Medium   Mixed Media

Brief   To create a fictional lost and found poster as a
response to an online gallery brief.

Andy Potts
Redstar: Get Out Of London

Design

Medium   Digital

Brief   To Design cd artwork for London based band
Redstar's EP.

Commissioned by   Sam Stubbings

Client   Redstar

Andy Potts
Monkeyluv

Books

Medium   Digital

Brief   Wrap around book cover Design for humourous
anthropological study of the similarities between
monkey and human behaviour.

Commissioned by   Eleanor Crow

Client   Random House

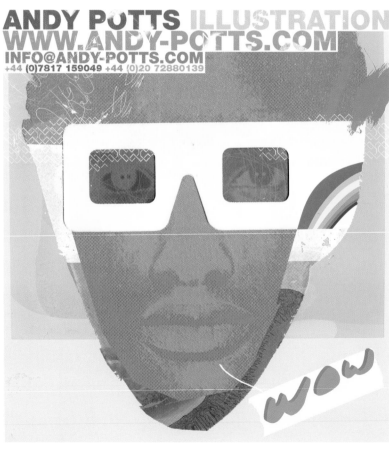

Andy Potts
Break Into Television

Design

Medium	Digital
Brief	To illustrate Channel 4 recruitment flier for television researchers aimed at ethnic minorities.
Commissioned by	James Chambers
Client	4 Creative
Commissioned for	Channel 4

Andy Potts
Bubby 3D

Self-Promotion

Medium	Mixed Media
Brief	To create a self promotional mail-out card.

Andy Potts

Hunter S Thompson

Editorial

Medium	Mixed Media
Brief	To illustrate Hunter S Thompson for a tribute article on the recently deceased Gonzo journalist and icon.
Commissioned by	Jason Horton
Client	Modart Magazine

Russell Cobb
RAM 2 (Random Access Memory)

Self-Promotion

Medium   Acrylic

Brief   Spread from a self promotion booklet mapping
the artist's inspirations, influences and obsessions.
Image two: Diagrams and Memories.

Russell Cobb
Passing Of Time

Self-Promotion

Medium   Acrylic

Brief   One of a series of self promotion cards. A playful
take on the passing of time while waiting for the
next commission to arrive.

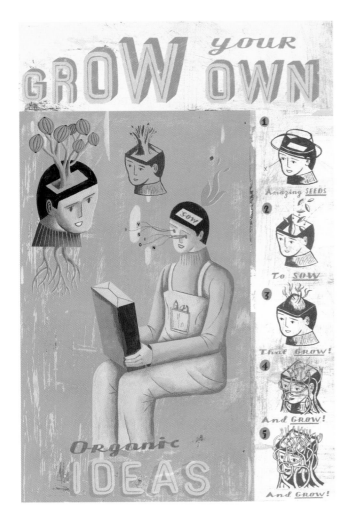

Russell Cobb

Grow Your Own Ideas

Self-Promotion

Medium	Acrylic
Brief	One of a series of self promotion cards playing on the idea of buying, cultivating and growing original ideas from organic seeds.

Russell Cobb

The Bumper Fiction Issue

Editorial

Medium	Acrylic
Brief	To produce a cover image for the Guardian Review magazine. Ten exlcusive new stories for summer.
Commissioned by	Pauline Doyle
Client	The Guardian
Commissioned for	The Guardian Review

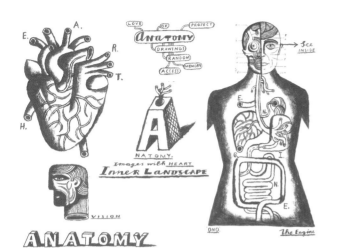

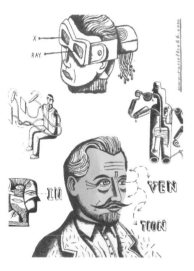

	Russell Cobb			**Russell Cobb**
	RAM 1 (Random Access Memory)			RAM 3 (Random Access Memory)
	Self-Promotion			**Self-Promotion**
Medium	Acrylic		Medium	Acrylic
Brief	Spread from a self promotion booklet mapping the artist's inspirations, influences and obsessions. Image one: Inventions, Anatomy and Autumn.		Brief	Spread from a self promotion booklet mapping the artist's inspirations, influences and obsessions. Image three: Imagination and Design.

Carol Seatory
Breakfast

Books

Medium	Mixed Media
Brief	From "The Tree" by Ken Lawrence, a story book for 7-9 year old children; in progress, as yet unpublished.
Commissioned by	Ken Lawrence

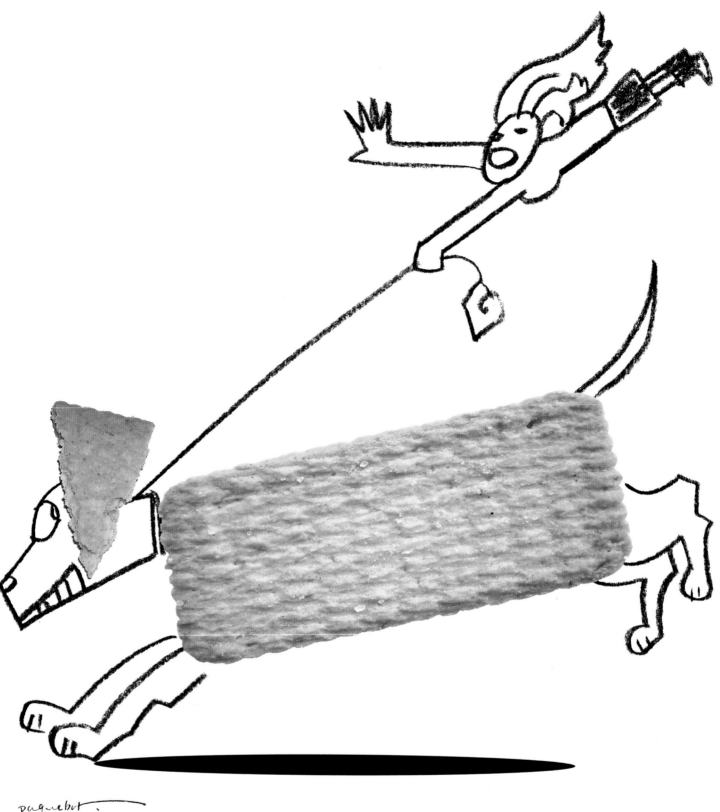

Paquebot
Victim Of Carbohydrate Craving

Editorial

Medium	Digital
Brief	Create an image about carbohydrate craving and show its effect on the victim.
Commissioned by	Maria Rodriguez
Client	Sainsbury's Magazine

Satoshi Kambayashi
Kyoto Treaty Effect

Editorial

Medium	Digital
Brief	Kyoto treaty does not necessarily mean a straight jacket on member state's greenhouse gas emissions.
Commissioned by	Una Corrigan
Client	The Economist Group
Commissioned for	The Economist

Paquebot
Money Game

Self-Promotion

Medium	Digital
Brief	Money has taken the soul of football.

Paquebot

Freudian 1

Self-Promotion

Medium   Digital

Brief   Illustrate a Freudian symbolism (cigar).

Paquebot

Freudian 2

Self-Promotion

Medium   Digital

Brief   Illustrate a Freudian symbolism (cigar).

Paquebot
No Pain, No Comedy

Self-Promotion

Medium	Digital
Brief	Best comedy always comes from personal pain.

Images 30

Greg Morgan
Diversity For Development

Design

Medium	Mixed Media
Brief	To illustrate the concept of biodiversity as a source of sustainable agricultural development.
Commissioned by	Dr Jeremy Cherfas
Client	IPGRI

Hanna Melin
No Sex Please

Editorial

Medium	Mixed Media
Brief	To illustrate an article about the growing popularity of a pledge card which when signed confirms that the owner will not have sex until marriage. The cards pose a problem for gays and lesbians in the United States who are not allowed to marry.
Commissioned by	Jane Czyzselska
Client	Diva Magazine

Images 30

Richard Levesley

Bear

Self-Promotion

Medium	Digital
Brief	A response to an article that explains how to react when confronted with a bear.

Richard Levesley

Lines Are Slimming

Self-Promotion

Medium	Digital
Brief	Taking a slimming method and adding my own sense of humour to make you look at it from a fresh perspective.

Richard Levesley

Fred Dibnah

Self-Promotion

Medium	Digital
Brief	Imagine how Fred Dibnah became interested in steam engines. Portrait of him on his first toy steam engine.

Richard Levesley
Chewy

Self-Promotion

Medium | Digital

Brief | To take trivia facts from celebrities lives and to convey the humour of the situation using word and image.

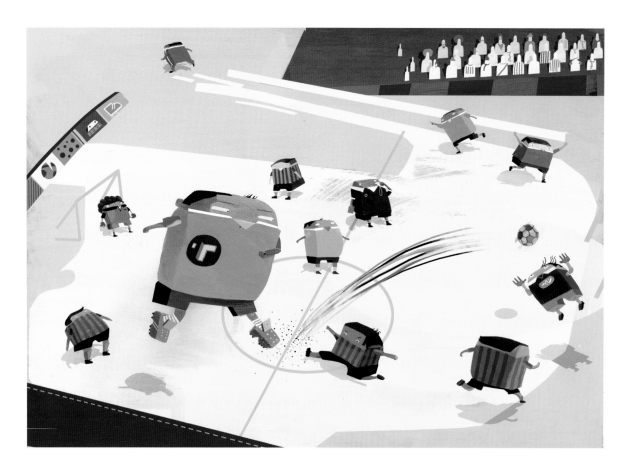

Graham Carter
Once Apon A Time

Self-Promotion

Medium   Mixed Media

Brief   To produce a series of images as a reaction to a
selection of fairytale stories written by Staffordshire
school children.

Graham Carter
Office Play

Editorial

Medium   Digital

Brief   To illustrate an article about anthropology in
the workplace.

Commissioned by   Andrew Lee

Client   Financial Times

Commissioned for   Cover of Saturday FT Magazine.

Stephen Knowles
Pyong Yang

Self-Promotion

Medium	Mixed Media
Brief	To create a mock propaganda poster for the Pyong Yang Film Festival.

Richard Johnson
The Snow March

Books

Medium	Acrylic
Brief	Illustrate 'Aesop's Fables', an 80 page children's book with 8 separate stories. Image should depict the wolf watching the band of pilgrims in the snow.
Commissioned by	Eliz Huseyin
Client	Kingfisher Publishing
Commissioned for	Aesop's Fables

Paul Bommer
Shoreditch Map April 2005 (detail)

Design

Medium   Digital
Brief   To illustrate in a unique way a map of the
                  Shoreditch/Hoxton area, capturing something of the
                  area's vibrancy and diversity.
Commissioned by   Rob Smith
Client   Universal Map Company
Commissioned for The Shoreditch Map

Paul Bommer
Happy Housewarming

Self-Promotion

Medium   Digital
Brief   A personal card for a friend's housewarming party.

Paul Bommer

No Murders, Mr Wilson, We're British

Editorial

Medium	Digital
Brief	An article on PM Harold Wilson's consideration of the possible need to assassinate Ugandan dictator Idi Amin.
Commissioned by	Roger Browning
Client	The Guardian

Paul Bommer

A Visit From St.Nick

Editorial

Medium	Digital
Brief	A piece of seasonal cheer!
Commissioned by	Paul Howlett
Client	The Guardian
Commissioned for	G2 Christmas Cartoon Special

Images 30

Paul Bommer
Hypochondria

Editorial

Medium	Digital
Brief	An article by Judy Rumbold on a hypochondriac's need for mild but exotic ailments and bugs.
Commissioned by	Pauline Doyle
Client	The Guardian
Commissioned for	The Guardian Weekend Magazine

Paul Bommer
Monster

Self-Promotion

Medium   Digital
Brief   A personal monster for the portfolio of the
           'monsters' illustrators' collective.

Paul Bommer
Darling Foods Of May

Editorial

Medium   Digital
Brief   A piece on three restaurants specializing in
                seasonal food, in this case the wonderful broad
                beans and asparagus of early May.
Commissioned by Gee Ibrahim
Client   The Guardian Guide
Commissioned for The Guardian Guide Food Page

Paul Bommer
Citron Dépressé

Self-Promotion

Medium   Digital
Brief   A Self-Promotional postcard with a twist
           of wordplay.

Jonas Bergstrand
Alfred Hitchcock Caricature

Self-Promotion

Medium   Digital
Brief   self promotion, caricature skills.

Jonas Bergstrand
Untitled

Advertising

Medium   Digital
Brief   Promotion image for the illustration agency CIA.
Commissioned by Louisa St.Pierre
Client   Central Illustration Agency (CIA)

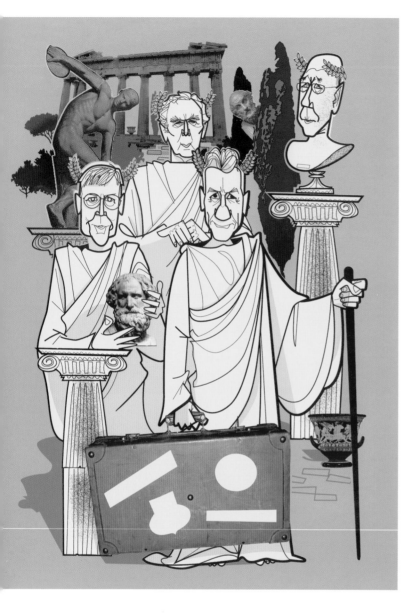

Jonas Bergstrand
Four Wise Men

Editorial

Medium	Digital
Brief	Every year, Saga Magazine lists the wisest people. This full page image (along with a handful of spot illustrations) supported that article.
Commissioned by	Paul Hayes-Watkins
Client	Saga Magazine

Jonas Bergstrand
Preparing For The Perfect Date

Editorial

Medium	Digital
Brief	Image about preparing for the perfect date. 1 out of 3 images commissioned for the article.
Commissioned by	Simon Robinson
Client	Orange Magazine

Becky Blair
Angels

Books

Medium	Mixed Media
Brief	To illustrate the following quote: "At the top is Metaton, the angel closest to God with seventy-two wings and innumerable eyes".
Commissioned by	Gail Jones
Client	Duncan Baird Publisher
Commissioned for	'Angels' Book

Brian Grimwood
Luther

Books

Medium	Mixed Media
Brief	One of forty spot illustrations for a book of W H Auden poems.
Commissioned by	Joe Whitlock Blundell
Client	The Folio Society
Commissioned for	W H Auden Poems

Brian Grimwood
Devil Head

Books

Medium	Mixed Media
Brief	One of forty spot illustrations for a book of W H Auden poems.
Commissioned by	Joe Whitlock Blundell
Client	The Folio Society
Commissioned for	W H Auden Poems

Brian Grimwood
Pan And Sow

Books

Medium	Mixed Media
Brief	One of forty spot illustrations for a book of W H Auden poems.
Commissioned by	Joe Whitlock Blundell
Client	The Folio Society
Commissioned for	W H Auden Poems

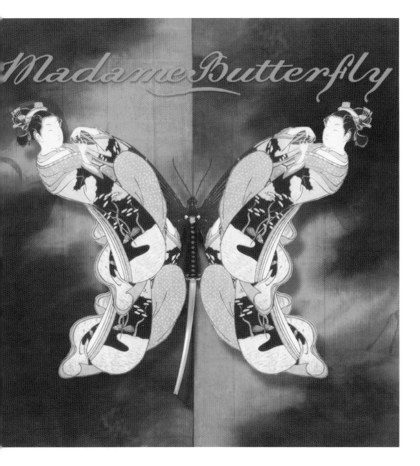

Barry Downard
Madame Butterfly

Advertising

Medium	Mixed Media
Brief	Create an eye-catching visual for the opera "Madame Butterfly".
Commissioned by	Catherine Guin
Client	Cleveland Opera

Stan Eales
Leather, Lace PVC and Chintz

Self-Promotion

Medium	Mixed Media
Brief	The image is from a book entitled "Modern World" which discusses how the old and the new are contrasted in contemporary society.

1st

1991 **Norton F.1** road version of a race winner

40

1969 **BSA Rocket 3** early three cylinder 'superbike'

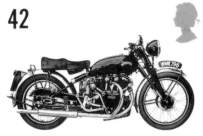

42

1949 **Vincent Black Shadow** fastest standard motorcycle

47

1938 **Triumph Speed Twin** two cylinder innovation

60

1930 **Brough Superior** bespoke luxury motorcycle

68

1914 **Royal Enfield** small engined motor bicycle

	Michael English			**David Bromley**
	Motorcycles			After Arafat
	Design			**Editorial**
Medium	Mixed Media		Medium	Scraperboard
Brief	To capture the detail and beauty of British motorcycles, by portraying production line models from 1914 to present day.		Brief	This accompanied an article on Arafat's death. The way was now clear for elections although this was not going to be an easy task.
Commissioned by	Catharine Brandy, Ian Chilvers, Jane Ryan		Commissioned by	Brana Radovic
Client	Royal Mail Group plc		Client	Financial Times
Commissioned for	Royal Mail Philatelic Design Team		Commissioned for	FT - Opinion Page

Max Ellis
Belle Du Jour

Editorial

Medium   Mixed Media

Brief   Produce an image to accompany the blog of a
                prostitute. A return to traditional media seemed
                appropriate for the subject.

Commissioned by Roger Browning

Client   The Guardian

Commissioned for G2 Supplement

Max Ellis
G. W. Bush Wasp

Self-Promotion

Medium   Digital

Brief   Part of a postcard exhibition for CIA. 'What I did
                last Summer'.

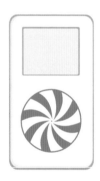

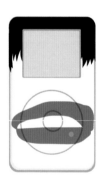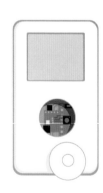

Ann Ellis
Party Of Two

Self-Promotion

Medium	Digital
Brief	In a bold and minimal snapshot portray two insular old ladies at a social gathering.

Chris Robson
iPods

Editorial

Medium	Digital
Brief	Following the U2 Limited Edition iPod, a selection for other musicians.
Commissioned by	Jason Simmons
Client	Dennis Publishing
Commissioned for	MacUser

Jill Calder
Sudoku Wine

Editorial

Medium	Mixed Media
Brief	Illustrate a wine article in which the writer compared compiling a wine list to solving a Sudoku puzzle.
Commissioned by	Bruno Haward
Client	The Guardian
Commissioned for	The Guardian Weekend Magazine

Mark Hudson
New Year's Day

Editorial

Medium	Digital
Brief	A page header for New Year's Day, heralding the fresh dawn of a brand new day.
Commissioned by	Alex Nicholas
Client	Radio Times
Commissioned for	Radio Times Xmas Issue

Mark Hudson
War Forecast

Self-Promotion

Medium	Digital
Brief	Can powerful software really forecast the outcome of armed conflict? Unused illustration for the Economist.
Commissioned by	Una Corrigan
Client	Economist Magazine
Commissioned for	Economist Special Feature

And something that really
puts the wind in their sails

Is finding the clippings
of all ten toe-nails.

Jan Bowman
St Mark's Place, Manhattan

Self-Promotion

Medium   Digital
Brief   Drawn from life.

Ruth Martin
Toenail Collection

Self-Promotion

Medium   Collage
Brief   Page idea for a children's picture book,
            'Nook + Cranny + Crevice, their hound'
            - who collect little grubby things lying around.

Andrew Selby
In England's Green And Pleasant Lands

Design

Medium	Digital
Brief	Illustration to promote British illustrators working for American clients.
Commissioned by	Charles Hively
Client	3x3 Magazine
Commissioned for	3x3: The Journal Of Contemporary Illustation

Nicholas Street
End Of The Word

Self-Promotion

Medium	Mixed Media
Brief	Self-promotional editorial illustrating the dominance of pictorial language over text throughout history.

Michael Bramman
Flood
Design

Medium   Acrylic
Brief   Show flooding on park land.
Commissioned by Ben Weaver
Client   Sheffield International Documentary Festival

Michael Bramman
Selfridges/Birmingham
Self-Promotion

Medium   Acrylic
Brief   Visit location, make notes for final painting.
              (abandoned project).
Commissioned by Catherine Brandy
Client   Royal Mail

Brian Cronin
Chinese Boy
Advertising

Medium   Mixed Media
Brief   Image for a fast food delivery company. They
              wanted to show the food and give over a
              traditionally Chinese feel.
Commissioned by Georgie Fountain
Client   20/20
Commissioned for Deliverence

Images 30

George Boorujy
WG Sebald In Corsica

Editorial

Medium	Mixed Media
Brief	Portrait of WG Sebald - a travel writer. Unfinished extract on Corsica.
Commissioned by	Roger Browning
Client	The Guardian
Commissioned for	The Guardian Review

Marco Ventura
The Last Post

Editorial

Medium	Acrylic
Brief	Portrait of TS Elliott - piece on his lost letters kept by his widow.
Commissioned by	Roger Browning
Client	The Guardian
Commissioned for	The Guardian Review

Lizzie Harper
Plate For Wildflower Guide

Books

Medium	Watercolour
Brief	Botanically accurate illustration of British wildflowers for guide, to scale with associated details.
Commissioned by	Helen Brocklehurst
Client	Harper Collins
Commissioned for	Wildflower Guide of Britain and North Europe

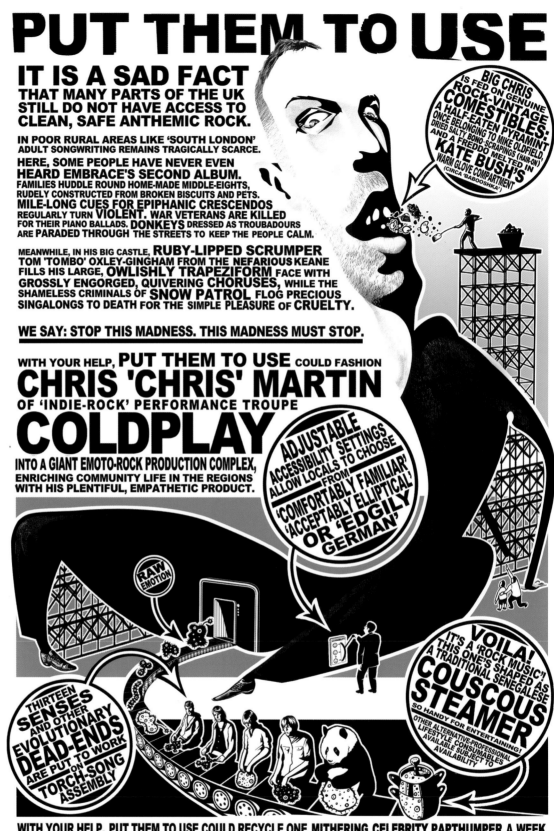

Stephen Collins
Promo Postcard: Chris Martin

Self-Promotion

Medium   Digital

Brief   One of a series of Self-Promotional caricature
postcards turning celebrities into useful objects.

Stephen Collins
Jamie Cullum

Editorial

Medium   Digital

Brief   To illustrate both a restaurant review and an
interview with Jamie Cullum set in London's
Coq d'Argent.

Commissioned by   Helen Whitley-Niland

Client   GQ Magazine

Stephen Collins
Gay Hitler

Editorial

Medium   Digital

Brief   A series of Village People-style illustrations for a
feature on historical icons who may have been gay.

Commissioned by   Lisa Kilpatrick

Client   Attitude Magazine

Stephen Collins
Gay Churchill

Editorial

Medium	Digital
Brief	A series of Village People-style illustrations for a feature on historical icons who may have been gay.
Commissioned by	Lisa Kilpatrick
Client	Attitude Magazine

	Jonny Hannah
	Swingers
	Books

Medium   Mixed Media

Brief   To give the endpapers for a book on jazz a
            jazzy feel.

Commissioned by   Deirdre McDermott

Client   Walker Books

	Jonny Hannah
	Cab-Aret?
	Editorial

Medium   Digital

Brief   For an article about how karaoke equipment has
            been installed in a cab in Morpeth, Northumberland
            as a calming influence on late night drinkers.

Commissioned by   Martin Colyer

Client   Reader's Digest Magazine

	Jonny Hannah
	Go! Rocket Man, Go!
	Self-Promotion

Medium   Mixed Media

Brief   To promote a superhero for my private press.

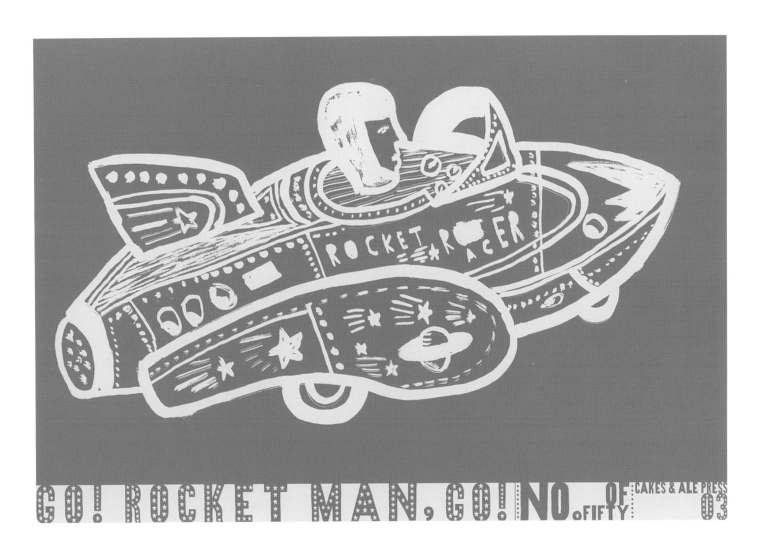

GO! ROCKET MAN, GO! NO. OF FIFTY CAKES & ALE PRESS 03

Jonny Hannah
The India House

Books

Medium	Collage
Brief	Illustrate a book about a family returning to England, in the fifties, after living in India for many years.
Commissioned by	Eleanor Crowe
Client	Jonathan Cape
Commissioned for	Random House

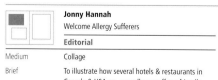

Jonny Hannah
Welcome Allergy Sufferers

Editorial

Medium   Collage
Brief   To illustrate how several hotels & restaurants in
            Canada & USA are now allergy sufferer friendly.
Commissioned by   Cinders Mcleod
Client   Toronto Globe & Mail

Jonny Hannah
The Cakes & Ale Shooting Gallery.

Self-Promotion

Medium   Collage
Brief   To promote my company for an exhibition using
            existing artwork.
Commissioned by   Nightingale Project
Client   Kensington & Chelsea Mental Health Project
Commissioned for   Nightingale Project

Glen McBeth
Diary Images 1

Self-Promotion

Medium   Mixed Media
Brief   The first of a continuing series of diary pages
            which includes life events, references to current
            commissioned illustration jobs, and general doodles.

113

Paul Wearing
David Ogilvy (Mid Career)

Design

Medium	Digital
Brief	One in a series of 3 portraits of David Ogilvy showing him in mid career for 8 foot high mural in O&M's offices.
Commissioned by	Meghan DeBruler
Client	Ogilvy & Mather, Chicago

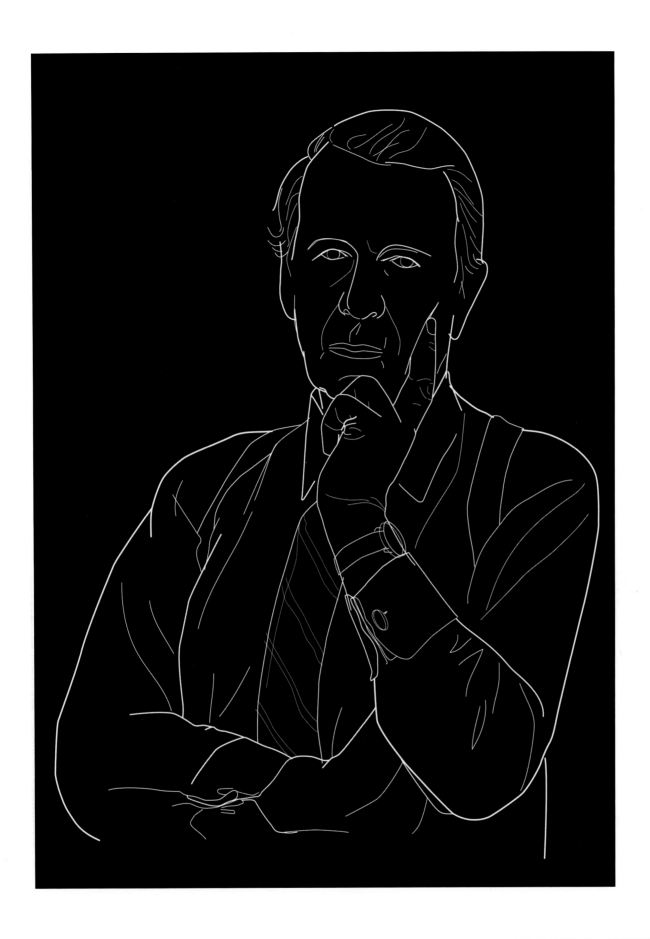

Paul Wearing
David Ogilvy (Later Years)

Design

Medium   Digital

Brief   One in a series of 3 portraits of David Ogilvy
                showing him in later years for 8 foot high mural in
                O&M's ofices.

Commissioned by Meghan DeBruler

Client   Ogilvy & Mather, Chicago

Paul Wearing
You Are What You Think

Editorial

Medium	Digital
Brief	Illustration for feature about how chemicals in the brain react. How we build up our own neuro net of nerve cells over years and how difficult it is to unattach them and change behavioral patterns.
Commissioned by	Gary Cochran
Client	The Telegraph Group
Commissioned for	Telegraph on Saturday Magazine

Paul Wearing
"The Stronger Option"

Design

Medium	Digital
Brief	Starting with the strap line "The Stronger Option" create an illustration that conveys overwhelming operational strength that Brit has achieved over it's competitors.
Commissioned by	Michael Mattinson
Client	SimplifyDesign
Commissioned for	Brit Insurance

maddie collection

Sport your style with finesse in a sweet selection of athletic footwear,
apparel and accessories perfectly detailed to mix, match and go.

  exclusively at Finish Line

For the Finish Line nearest you call toll-free 1-877-777-FINL   www.finishline.com/maddie

vault49

Maddie Purple

Advertising

Medium	Mixed Media
Brief	To show the movement, energy and excitement of Nike's new product range.
Commissioned by	Gary Vossenkemper
Client	Cinco Company
Commissioned for	Nike USA

vault49

Digit Magazine Cover 3

Editorial

Medium	Mixed Media
Brief	To show the successful integration of typography and illustration, specifically through the medium of Adobe Illustrator and Photoshop CS, in keeping with the magazine's lead article.
Commissioned by	Chris Hodgson
Client	Digit
Commissioned for	Digit Magazine

 Laura Scott
S Is For... A Celestial Body

Self-Promotion

Medium   Mixed Media

Brief   From a series of self-initiated illustrations exploring
the theme 'S is for... '.

Sara Creson
Noisy Silence

Self-Promotion

Medium   Digital

Brief   To discuss the idea that one can experience silence
in a non-silent environment.

Images 30

Ann Elson
Playboy

Self-Promotion

Medium   Mixed Media

Brief   Playboy - a new breed

Fossil Glanville
Torino 2006

Self-Promotion

Medium   Digital

Brief   Competition for Winter Olympics 2006 held in
Torino to promote the games.

Fossil Glanville
New Architecture

Self-Promotion

Medium   Digital

Brief   SAA transport for London. To promote new
architecture by bus, tube and river.

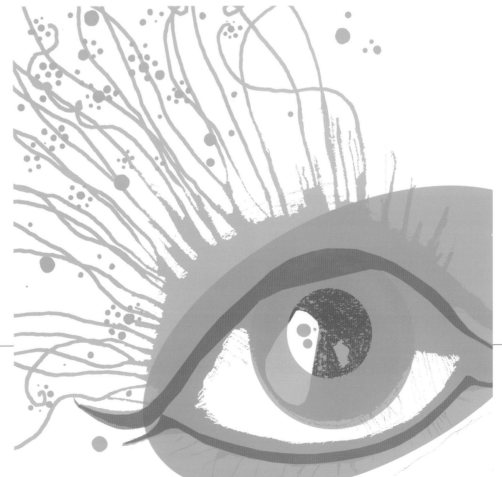

Fossil Glanville

The Elements: Earth

Self-Promotion

Medium	Digital
Brief	Using the eye to evoke four different elements: earth, fire, water and air.

Beach
Moaning Magenta

Editorial

Medium	Mixed Media
Brief	Illustrate an article about difficult clients from a builder's point of view.
Commissioned by	Jon Farley
Client	The Daily Telegraph
Commissioned for	Telegraph Property

Beach
Steamboat Robot

Design

Medium	Mixed Media
Brief	One of a series of images for a band's website depicting their story in allegorical form.
Commissioned by	Rhys Williams
Client	Amber Gate

Beach
Super Monkey Skate

Self-Promotion

Medium	Digital
Brief	An oblique take on the superhero theme created to amuse a class of primary school children in Big Arts Week.

The Guardian 02.07.05 ❧ *guardian.co.uk/books*

Review

The perfectionist

Julian Barnes on the restless genius of Frank O'Connor

124

Thea Brine
Frank O'Connor

Editorial

Medium	Mixed Media
Brief	Portray the writer, his character and working methods: perfectionism and continual re-drafting. Reflect the time he was writing -1930's - 1950's.
Commissioned by	Roger Browning
Client	The Guardian
Commissioned for	The Guardian Review Cover

Oliver Harud
Zarastien

Self-Promotion

Medium	Digital
Brief	Character study for portfolio targeted at gaming industry.

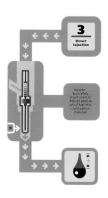

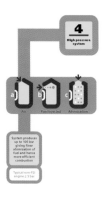

Peter Grundy
Save Fuel

Advertising

Medium | Digital
Brief | Create a diagram to show customers how VW cars save fuel.
Commissioned by | Nick Allsop
Client | DDB London
Commissioned for | VW

Peter Grundy
Trafalgar Stamps

Design

Medium | Digital
Brief | Show Battle of Trafalgar facts.
Commissioned by | Susan Gilson
Client | Royal Mail
Commissioned for | Trafalgar Anniversary

Karen Quinn

The Ivy Chronicles

I laughed delightedly with the wry laugh of a parent who had been there. ELIZABETH BUCHAN

Sarah Gibb
The Ivy Chronicles

Books

Medium	Mixed Media
Brief	To illustrate cover.
Commissioned by	Jeremy Butcher
Client	Simon & Schuster Ltd

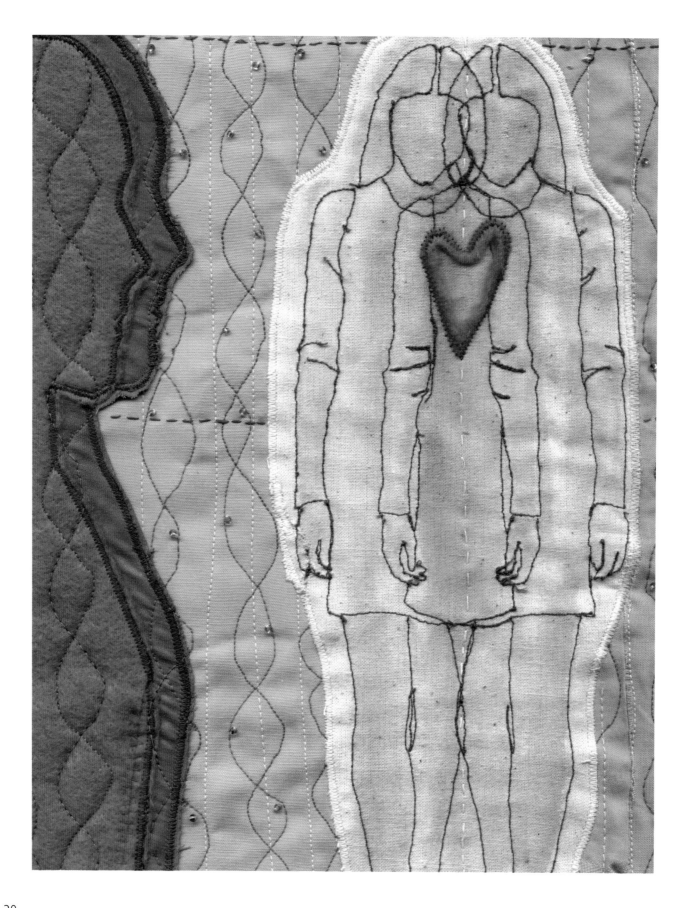

Lucille Toumi
Seeing Double

Self-Promotion

Medium	Stitched Textile Collage
Brief	The unique relationship and daily life of identical twins, who live identical lives in every way.

David Lupton
Untitled

Editorial

Medium	Pen and Ink (line and wash)
Brief	To create an illustration to open a special on the complex relationship between animals and humans.
Commissioned by	Craig Mackie
Client	New Scientist

Frances Castle
Wired World

Self-Promotion

Medium	Digital
Brief	Self-initiated promotional work to appeal to the art directors of computer magazines.

NERVOUS ENERGY

Darren is paranoid that you don't like him

Tom Gaul
Tommy Cooper

Self-Promotion

Medium   Mixed Media
Brief   Produce a self promotional, humourous, caricature
          of the comedian: Tommy Copper.

Jim Smith
Hello Darren Brand Cofee Cup

Self-Promotion

Medium   Mixed Media
Brief   From 'Rock Blondsky's Bad Ideas' (Self-Promotion).

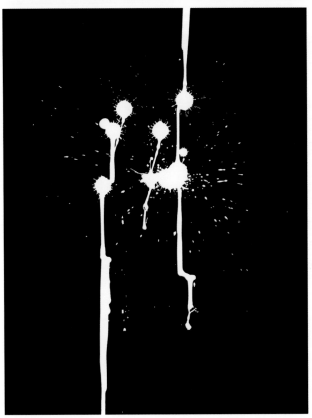

Ulla Puggaard
Darkroom 1

Editorial

Medium	Mixed Media
Brief	Story (1,2,3) commissioned for 2nd issue of S-publication, a bi-annual art-erotic magazine based in Copenhagen. The theme is open to contributers.
Commissioned by	Jens Stolze
Client	S Publication
Commissioned for	S Magazine Issue 2

Ulla Puggaard
Darkroom 3

Editorial

Medium	Mixed Media
Brief	Story (1,2,3) commissioned for 2nd issue of S-publication, a bi-annual art-erotic magazine based in Copenhagen. The theme is open to contributers.
Commissioned by	Jens Stolze
Client	S Publication
Commissioned for	S Magazine Issue 2

Michelle Thompson
New Architecture In London

Self-Promotion

Medium	Collage
Brief	To promote new architecture in London by tube, bus and river.
Commissioned by	SAA

Michelle Thompson
Incendiary

Editorial

Medium	Collage
Brief	Story set in 2005, aftermath of an explosion that kills 1000 Londoners, mainly Arsenal and Chelsea fans.
Commissioned by	Samuel Freeman
Client	Big Issue Magazine
Commissioned for	The Big Issue

Catell Ronca
Changing Tastes In Britain

Design

Medium	Mixed Media
Brief	To represent the ethnic mixture of the UK in a positive and engaging manner, through the universal theme of food.
Commissioned by	Jane Ryan, Catharine Brandy
Client	Royal Mail Group plc
Commissioned for	Royal Mail Philatelic Design Team

James Bourne

Aquatic Ape Theory

Self-Promotion

Medium   Mixed Media

Brief   To illustrate a theory. I chose the Aquatic Ape Theory which states that sea life played a major part in human evolution.

Lorna Apps-Woodland
A Million Different People

Editorial

Medium	Collage
Brief	A young amnesiac becomes someone new every week in the hope of finding her true self. (Radio play).
Commissioned by	Alex Nicholas
Client	Radio Times

Nick Radford

The Outside Set

Editorial

Medium	Mixed Media
Brief	Editorial Illustration (DPS) for article on how surfers used to be outsiders on the fringes of society. Leaving room for 800 words.
Commissioned by	Helen Gilchrist (editor)
Client	Stranger Magazine

Bee Willey
Down The Alley

Books

Medium   Mixed Media

Brief   Cats converging in the evening through the alleys
                of London, for a grand meeting with Felissima the
                celebrity cat.

Commissioned by Judith Escreet

Client   Frances Lincoln Publishing

Ella Tjader
Madonna/Virgo

Self-Promotion

Medium   Digital

Brief   Create Virgo sign illustration inspired by Art Deco &
                Art Nouveau. I wanted to portray an innocent and
                angelic girl on a strong flowery background.

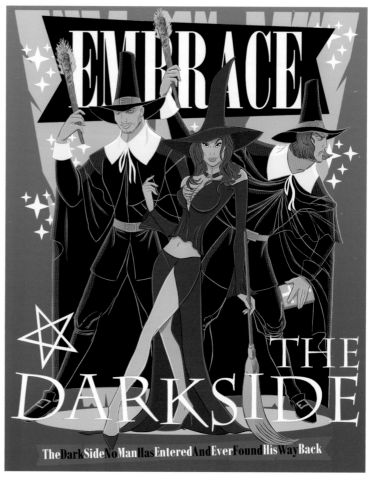

John Charlesworth

101 Essential Items That Any Self-Respecting
Criminal Genius Should Never Be Without

Self-Promotion

Medium	Digital
Brief	A Self-Promotional piece taken from a series of eight illustrations enitled "A lesson in bad taste".

John Charlesworth

Deliver Us From Evil

Self-Promotion

Medium	Digital
Brief	A speculative piece which trivialises the allure of the occult as a synthetic fashion statement.

Federico Gallo
Mask

Editorial

Medium	Mixed Media
Brief	To illustrate an article/discussion on Foucalt's theories about madness. The blurred make-up of an improbable pin-up, suggests the internal anxiety... the unbalance.
Commissioned by	
Client	Naked Punch KCL Press
Commissioned for	Naked Punch Magazine

Federico Gallo
WE, Dwellers

Editorial

Medium	Pen and Ink (line and wash)
Brief	To illustrate an article/interview "The politics of empire". 70 illustrations show busy citizens in daily activities. Together the 70 images form a portrait, a representation of fear.
Client	Naked Punch KCL Press
Commissioned for	Naked Punch Magazine

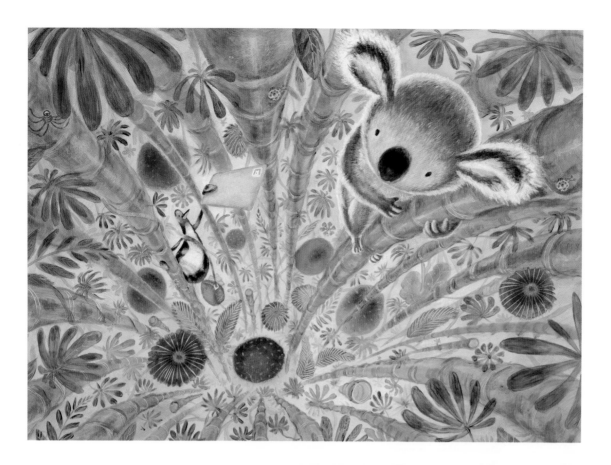

 Barry Ablett
Penguin Post

Self-Promotion

Medium   Acrylic

Brief   Illustrate a spread for my own picture book story.

 Bill Butcher
Attack

Editorial

Medium   Digital

Brief   To illustrate a journalists account of a violent
               attack on a woman in Washington DC seen through
               his eyes.

Commissioned by   Sara Wadsworth

Client   Financial Times

Commissioned for   FT Magazine

Bill Butcher

Toboggan 15th US

Design

Medium   Digital

Brief   To Design a poster for the Camden Maine Toboggan championships which is open to anybody and is highly dangerous in the USA.

Commissioned by   Greg Bokor

Client   Camden Maine

Commissioned for   Camden Maine Ski Resort

Giulio Iurissevich

The Elders

Self-Promotion

Medium   Digital

Brief   It was my idea for a rock band's CD cover and poster.

Henning Löhlein
Greg Looking For Bernadine

Books

Medium	Acrylic
Brief	Greg, a hero in sheep-skin, is looking for Bernardine in the forest.
Commissioned by	Paxmann
Client	Altberliner Verlag (Germany)
Commissioned for	Children's Book

Henning Löhlein
Cheeky Dog

Books

Medium	Acrylic
Brief	Cheeky dog, the main character, is up to all sorts of things in the house.
Commissioned by	Paxmann
Client	Altberliner Verlag (Germany)
Commissioned for	Children's Book

Henning Löhlein
School Register

Editorial

Medium	Mixed Media
Brief	Fingerprint recognition programs could have a wide use, such as in schools, to allow only registered persons access to the premises.
Client	The Guardian
Commissioned for	Online Supplement

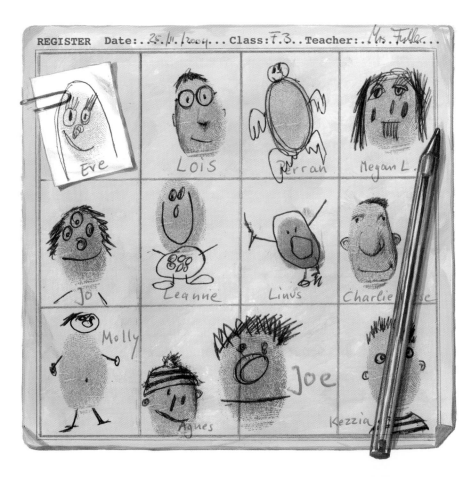

REGISTER Date: 25./11./2004... Class: F.3.. Teacher: Mrs. Fuller...

Eve

Lois

Perran

Megan L.

Jo

Leanne

Linus

Charlie Rose

Molly

Agnes

Joe

Kezzia

Henning Löhlein
The Food Chain

Self-Promotion

Medium	Acrylic
Brief	A book about Noah's Ark - dining on the ship.

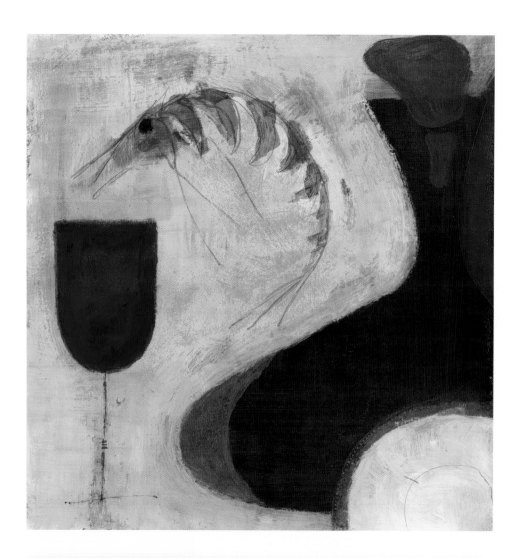

To some it's black and white.
To you it's many different colours.

Local Services | Forensic Services | Corporate Services

Eleanor Clark
Wine & Prawns

Self-Promotion

Medium — Mixed Media

Brief — Illustrate food.

Eleanor Clark
Consumer's Choice - Get It Before Her

Self-Promotion

Medium — Mixed Media

Brief — Illustrate supermarket manipulation & how our diet of supermarket products has brought about a loss in the real choices available.

Eleanor Clark
Untitled

Advertising

Medium — Mixed Media

Brief — Illustrate advertisement for art therapist recruitment poster.

Commissioned by — Duncan James

Client — Riley Advertising London

A. Richard Allen

Skip

Self-Promotion

Medium	Mixed Media
Brief	Self-Promotion.

A. Richard Allen

Movers

Editorial

Medium	Mixed Media
Brief	Article about a professional removals firm whose staff are described as being as co-ordinated as dancers in the Bolshoi ballet company.
Commissioned by	Mike Krage
Client	The Times
Commissioned for	The Times - Bricks & Mortar

James Fryer
The Good Company

Editorial

Medium	Acrylic
Brief	Companies aren't always as socially responsible as they make themselves out to be.
Commissioned by	Graeme James
Client	Economist
Commissioned for	The Economist Magazine

James Fryer
Untitled

Self-Promotion

Medium	Acrylic
Brief	Diagnosing necrotising fasciitis. Illustration pitch for a years front covers for the journal of wound care.
Commissioned by	Tracy Cowan
Client	EMAP Health Care Ltd
Commissioned for	Test Piece for Journal of Wound Care

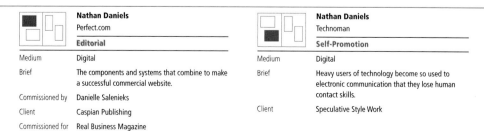

	Nathan Daniels			**Nathan Daniels**
	Perfect.com			Technoman
	Editorial			**Self-Promotion**
Medium	Digital		Medium	Digital
Brief	The components and systems that combine to make a successful commercial website.		Brief	Heavy users of technology become so used to electronic communication that they lose human contact skills.
Commissioned by	Danielle Salenieks		Client	Speculative Style Work
Client	Caspian Publishing			
Commissioned for	Real Business Magazine			

Nathan Daniels
Kids Real Food

Editorial

Medium	Digital
Brief	Article for modern children's magazine to encourage cooking and enjoying eating out real food (not fast food).
Commissioned by	John Tennant
Client	7 Publishing
Commissioned for	Kid's Magazine.

Nathan Daniels
Future House

Editorial

Medium	Digital
Brief	Practical technology for the house of the future that's available now.
Commissioned by	Graham Tuckwell
Client	Financial Times
Commissioned for	Financial Times Weekend

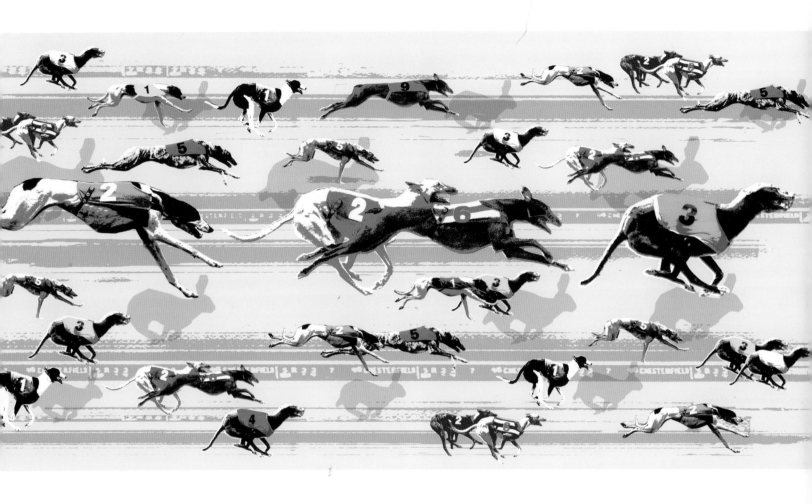

Tony Campbell
Greyhound

Design

Medium   Mixed Media

Brief   One of four artworks commissioned for a corporate
                identity illustrating the colours grey, green, pink
                and blue.

Commissioned by Gary Westlake

Client   Purple Design

Des Taylor

Thomas Pink Retro Christmas Promotion

Advertising

Medium	Mixed Media
Brief	To create illustrations for six window displays in a classic, sexy pin-up, girly magazine style.
Commissioned by	Emma Davidge
Client	Chameleon Visual
Commissioned for	Thomas Pink

Jake Abrams

'A'

Self-Promotion

Medium	Mixed Media
Brief	One of a set of illustrative type forms used for self promotion.

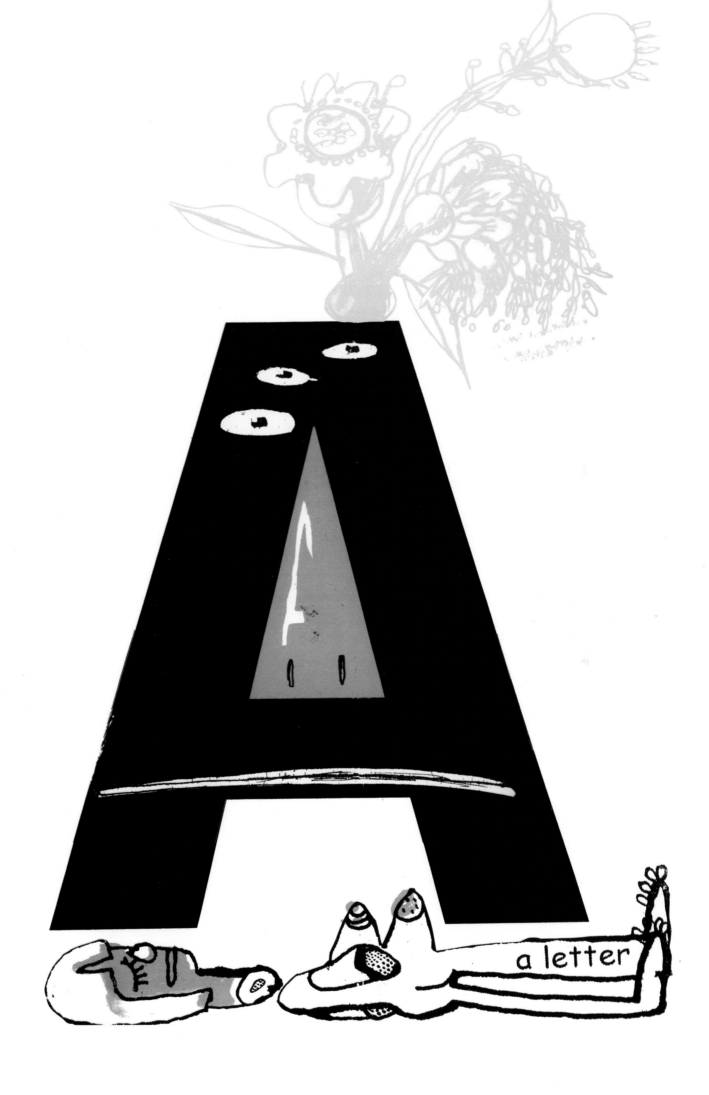

a letter

Matt Murphy
The Second Life Of Samuel Tyne

Books

Medium	Mixed Media
Brief	To produce a wrap around book jacket containing key elements from the book, including a bowler hat and blue jacket.
Commissioned by	Raquel Leis Rivera
Client	Time Warner Books

Matt Murphy

Woman On Her Way Home

Self-Promotion

Medium   Mixed Media

Brief   I liked the idea of the woman being at the end
of her journey, and yet at the start. What does she
do next?

George Hardie

Magic

Design

Medium   Mixed Media

Brief   "Show me magic and make it magical".
Solution: five interactive magic tricks.

Commissioned by   Tatham Design, Jane Ryan, Susan Gilson

Client   Royal Mail Group plc

Commissioned for   Royal Mail Philatelic Design Team

Christopher Wormell

Farm Animals

Design

Medium	Mixed Media
Brief	Represent ten farm animals within a graphic format that create pace across the range, supported by engaging packaging.
Commissioned by	Susan Gilson, Marcus James, Jason Godfrey, Jane Ryan
Client	Royal Mail Group plc
Commissioned for	Royal Mail Philatelic Design Team

Raymond Briggs

Christmas 2004

Design

Medium	Mixed Media
Brief	To represent the hardworking and warm spirit of the Father Christmas character, shown through him braving all weathers. The packaging further enhances the message.
Commissioned by	Jane Ryan, Marcus James, Ashted Dastor
Client	Royal Mail Group plc
Commissioned for	Royal Mail Philatelic Design Team

Alan Heighton

Leisure Logic

Self-Promotion

Medium	Digital
Brief	Self promotional work illustrating various characters carrying on with their personal leisure activities and persuits.

Images 30

Jane Webster
Marrakech Travel Cover

Editorial

Medium	Mixed Media
Brief	Illustrate the 5 areas of Marrakech in one image, souks, food markets, riad, Kazbar and Koutoubia from highest point of the city.
Commissioned by	Martin Harrison
Client	The Times Newspaper
Commissioned for	Travel Magazine

Jane Webster
Jack White Upholstery

Editorial

Medium	Mixed Media
Brief	Portrait of Jack White to support a feature concentrating upon his previous career as a furniture upholsterer.
Commissioned by	Declan Fahy
Client	Esquire Men's Magazine
Commissioned for	Esquire October 2005

Daniela Jaglenka Terrazzini
Little Red Riding Hood

Self-Promotion

Medium	Watercolour
Brief	To produce a series of illustrations depicting scenes from the story 'Little Red Riding Hood'.

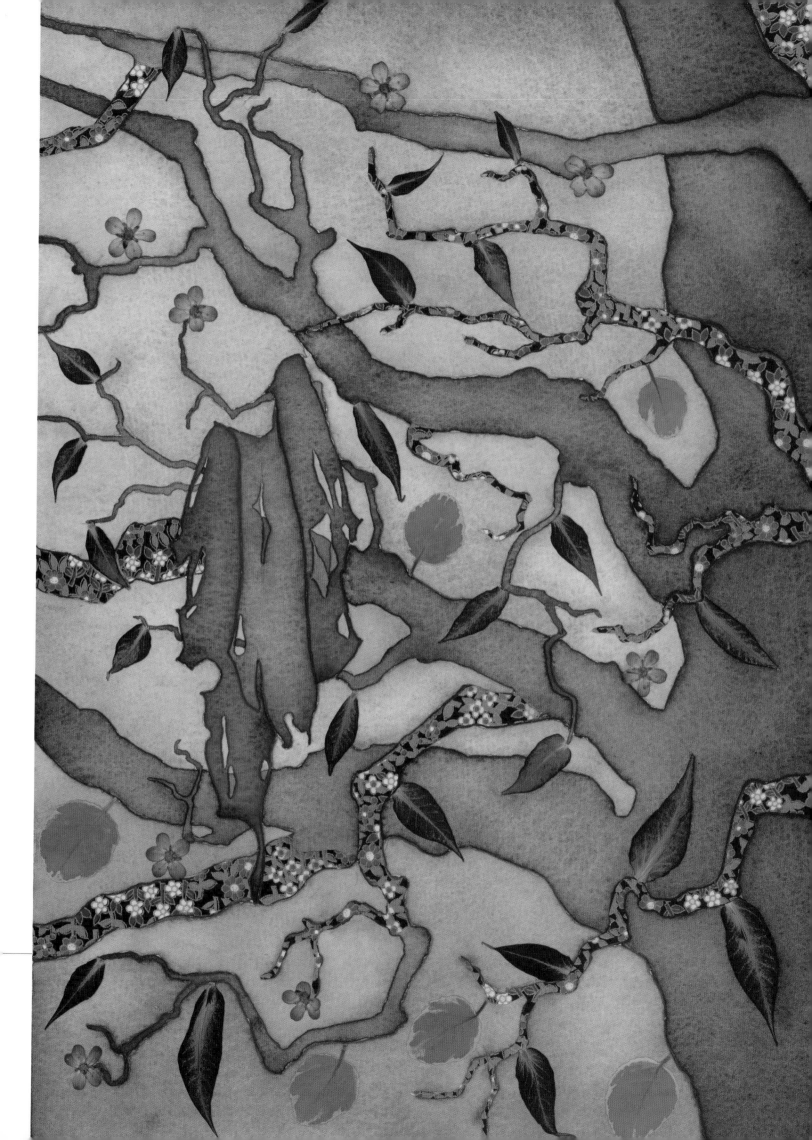

David Bray
Rapunzel

Editorial

Medium	Pen and Ink (line and wash)
Brief	Illustrate your favourite fairy tale.
Commissioned by	Carlos Serrat
Client	The Creator Studio
Commissioned for	The Creator Studio Magazine

Alison Lang
Penguin The Publisher

Editorial

Medium	Ink Brush and Digital
Brief	To illustrate the Penguin logo in the personality of founder, Allen Lane.
Commissioned by	Tim Shearring
Client	The Daily Telegraph

Rod Hunt
Angrybot

Self-Promotion

Medium   Digital

Brief   Produce a new promotional piece.

Rod Hunt
Abolish Automation

Editorial

Medium   Digital

Brief   Customers don't want to be treated like robots and neither do call centre staff. Proper training can add a human touch.

Commissioned by   Hannah Daw

Client   CMP Information

Commissioned for   Call Centre Focus Magazine

Matt Lee
Bad Skin

Editorial

Medium   Mixed Media

Brief   I've always had good skin but in the past months
                it's become blotchy. My pores have opened and my
                cheeks are often red and puffy.

Commissioned by   Pauline Doyle

Client   The Guardian

Commissioned for Weekend Magazine

Matt Lee
My Wife Linda

Editorial

Medium   Mixed Media

Brief   My wife Linda (61 yrs) has lost her sense of smell
                and taste following a cold four months ago. Do you
                have any suggestions?

Commissioned by   Pauline Doyle

Client   The Guardian

Commissioned for Weekend Magazine

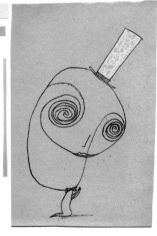

Matt Lee

Lord, Stay By Me

Self-Promotion

Medium   Mixed Media

Brief   From a series of 40 praying character drawings.
The aim was to abstract and develop the characters
through a singular theme.

Tania Konstant

Strange Coop

Self-Promotion

Medium   Digital

Brief   Inspired idea of a fictitious ligerie company called
"Strange Coop". Image also entered for animal
T-shirt graphic competition.

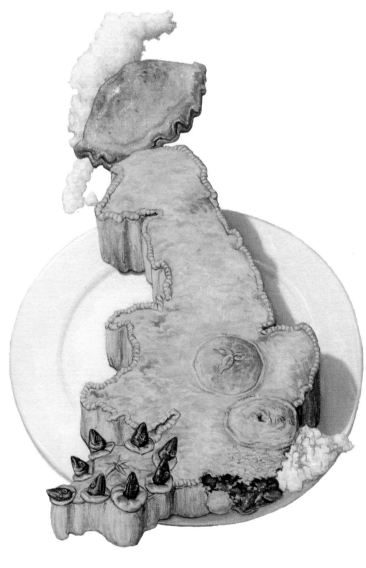

Jonathan Cusick
Private Passions - Stephen Fry

Editorial

Medium	Acrylic
Brief	A caricature of Stephen Fry to illustrate his appearance on Radio 3's Private Passions on Boxing Day.
Commissioned by	Alex Nicholas
Client	BBC Worldwide Ltd
Commissioned for	Radio Times

Jonathan Cusick
Who Ate All The Pies?

Editorial

Medium	Acrylic
Brief	A map of the country as a pie, showing regions as the relevant local pies for a Radio 4 Series surveying pies of Britain.
Commissioned by	Alex Nicholas
Client	BBC Worldwide Ltd
Commissioned for	Radio Times

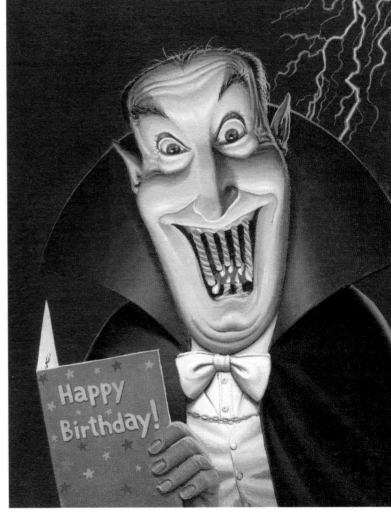

Jonathan Cusick

Santa

Self-Promotion

Medium   Acrylic

Brief   Design for Self-Promotional christmas card
              featuring a traditional Santa.

Jonathan Cusick

Dracula's 100th Birthday

Self-Promotion

Medium   Acrylic

Brief   A piece celebrating the centenary of
              Bram Stoker's novel.

Ian Pollock

Marcel Proust

Editorial

Medium	Mixed Media
Brief	Portrait of Marcel Proust 'Writers on Music - feature'.
Client	BBC Music Magazine.

Ian Pollock

It Sucks

Advertising

Medium	Mixed Media
Brief	Poster for the "Vampire" exhibition at the Edinburgh Dungeon.
Commissioned by	Rob Hammond
Client	Real Adventure
Commissioned for	The Edinburgh Dungeon

Jonathan Burton
Verdi

Editorial

Medium   Mixed Media

Brief   Composer of the Month. To characterise Verdi
                showing his Operatic imagination and his
                Italian roots.

Commissioned by   Chris Barker

Client   Haymarket Publishing

Commissioned for Classic FM Magazine

Jonathan Burton
Bliar

Editorial

Medium   Pen and Ink (line and wash)

Brief   To set the scene for an article based on the
                possibilty of Tony Blair being arrested for
                impeachment at the House of Commons.

Commissioned by   Andrew Lee

Client   The Financial Times

Commissioned for Financial Times Magazine

Jonathan Burton
Dvorak

Editorial

Medium	Mixed Media
Brief	Composer of the Month. To characterise Dvorak best known for the 'Hovis' theme in situ on Gold Hill whilst showing his Prague roots.
Commissioned by	Chris Barker
Client	Haymarket Publishing
Commissioned for	Classic FM Magazine

passing down below...the straggling fields
....of corn....barley....river-ford...

Sue Jarman
Ghosts And Shadows 2

Self-Promotion

Medium   Mixed Media

Brief   Interpret as a series of images the poem 'Ghosts
              and shadows' - based on myths, shadows and
              legends - exhibit the work as an installation.

Sue Jarman
Ghosts And Shadows 4

Self-Promotion

Medium   Mixed Media

Brief   Interpret as a series of images the poem 'Ghosts
              and Shadows' - based on myths, shadows and
              legends - exhibit the work as an installation.

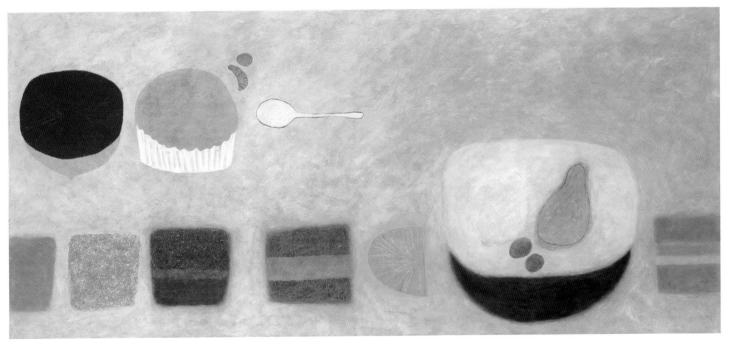

Sue Jarman

Ghosts And Shadows 1

Self-Promotion

Medium	Mixed Media
Brief	Interpret as a series of images the poem 'Ghosts and Shadows' - based on myths, shadows and legends - exhibit the work as an installation.

Sue Williams

Naughty But Nice

Design

Medium	Mixed Media
Brief	Explore these words within an image that can work both as a whole and as cropped sections: discerning, hedonistic, wise, health conscious, greedy, desserts.
Commissioned by	Georgie Fountain
Client	20/20
Commissioned for	Deliverance

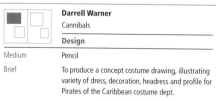

Darrell Warner

Cannibals

Design

Medium	Pencil
Brief	To produce a concept costume drawing, illustrating variety of dress, decoration, headress and profile for Pirates of the Caribbean costume dept.
Commissioned by	Penny Rose
Costume Designer	Pirates of the Caribbean 2/3
Commissioned for	Disney Pictures

Lara Harwood

Cures For Hair Loss

Editorial

Medium	Mixed Media
Brief	An article on the increase of young women suffering from hair loss, and suggested cures such as accupuncture and herbs.
Commissioned by	J Christie
Client	The Independent
Commissioned for	The Independent on Sunday

Lara Harwood

Changes And New Tricks

Editorial

Medium	Mixed Media
Brief	An article on change and evolving new practices in management.
Commissioned by	Anne Braybon
Client	Management Today

Lara Harwood

Turkey

Design

Medium	Mixed Media
Brief	One of six meat packaging labels for Booths food shops. This one is for turkey products.
Commissioned by	Angelo Ferrara
Client	Wolff Olins
Commissioned for	Booths

Dan Williams
Vizla

Self-Promotion

Medium   Pen and Ink (line and wash)

Brief   One of a series of images drawn on site at Crufts
2005, documenting the eccentricities of English life.

Dan Williams
Staffs

Self-Promotion

Medium   Pen and Ink (line and wash)

Brief   One of a series of images drawn on site at Crufts
2005. Part of the illustrators ongoing project to
document the eccentricities of English life.

Dan Williams
Going Home

Self-Promotion

Medium   Pen and Ink (line and wash)

Brief   One of a series of images drawn on site at Crufts
2005, documenting the eccentricities of English life.

Mr Stamp was acting oddly too, when Billy passed him. He was taking all the letters from the houses and putting them back into the postbox! Billy was surprised that Mr Stamp had not said hello and wondered if he'd done something wrong.

	Olivier Kugler	
	Last Flight Of The Little Prince	
	Editorial	
Medium	Digital	
Brief	To illustrate the story of Antoine de Saint Exupery, creator of 'The Little Prince' whose plane disappeared off the coast of France during World War II.	
Commissioned by	Martin Colyer	
Client	Reader's Digest Magazine	

	Sam McCullen	
	Billy Back-To-Front	
	Books	
Medium	Mixed Media and Digital	
Brief	Double page spread from a children's picture book, showing the lead character, Billy, walking through a back to front world.	
Commissioned by	Anne McNeil	
Client	Hodder Children's Books	

Simon Stern
Standing Up To The Bear

Design

Medium   Mixed Media

Brief   One of nine illustrations for fund manager's
promo - "investors are seeing off the bear market".
F&C is "Foreign&Colonial" hence old fashioned
look of the man.

Commissioned by   Phil Keevil

Client   Keevil, Barton, Kershaw

Commissioned for   F&C Management Ltd.

Simon Stern
Boxing The Bear

Design

Medium   Mixed Media

Brief   One of nine illustrations for fund manager's
promo - "investors are seeing off the bear market".
F&C is "Foreign&Colonial" hence old fashioned
look of the man.

Commissioned by   Phil Keevil

Client   Keevil, Barton, Kershaw

Commissioned for   F&C Management Ltd.

183

Simon Stern
Silent Night

Self-Promotion

Medium   Mixed Media

Brief   A personal christmas card to send to friends
            and clients.

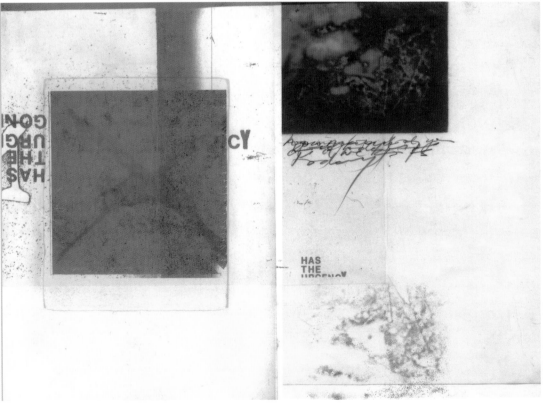

Dominic Trevett

373 Things To Do With Your Degree

Editorial

Medium	Digital
Brief	Create a cover showing the possible uses a science degree may have.
Commissioned by	Alison Lawn
Client	New Scientist

Dominic Trevett

Chocolate Biscuit Tree

Editorial

Medium	Digital
Brief	Illustrate a mystery text.
Commissioned by	Linda Elander
Client	Sunday Times Magazine

Jules A. Sykes

Urgency

Self-Promotion

Medium	Mixed Media
Brief	Response to a written piece concerning the loss of passion in relationships when things become familiar and comfortable.

Yellow iris, ribwort, spear thistle, foxglove, creeping thistle, common toadflax, corn poppy.

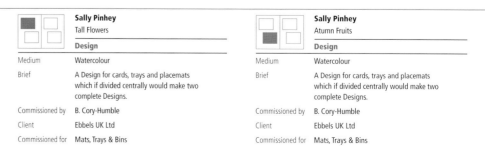

	Sally Pinhey			**Sally Pinhey**
	Tall Flowers			Atumn Fruits
	Design			**Design**
Medium	Watercolour		Medium	Watercolour
Brief	A Design for cards, trays and placemats which if divided centrally would make two complete Designs.		Brief	A Design for cards, trays and placemats which if divided centrally would make two complete Designs.
Commissioned by	B. Cory-Humble		Commissioned by	B. Cory-Humble
Client	Ebbels UK Ltd		Client	Ebbels UK Ltd
Commissioned for	Mats, Trays & Bins		Commissioned for	Mats, Trays & Bins

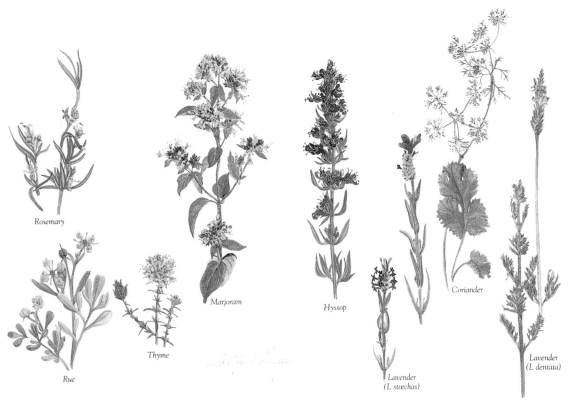

Rosemary

Marjoram

Hyssop

Coriander

Thyme

Rue

Lavender
(L stœchas)

Lavender
(L dentata)

		Sally Pinhey				**David Lyttleton**
		Herbs				Great Comedians
		Design				**Editorial**
Medium		Watercolour		Medium		Digital
Brief		A Design for cards, trays and placemats which if divided centrally would make two complete Designs.		Brief		Portraits of eight great comedians: Eric Morcambe, Billy Connolly, Dame Edna Everidge, Robin Williams, Paul Merton, Harry Hill, Eddie Izzard and Jasper Carrott.
Commissioned by		B. Cory-Humble		Commissioned by		Martin Colyer
Client		Ebbels UK Ltd		Client		Reader's Digest Magazine
Commissioned for		Mats, Trays & Bins				

 Sara Hayward
Church On The Severn

Books

Medium	Oils
Brief	Illustration for a book entitled 'Secular Lives, Sacred Hearts' by Alan Billings. The painting depicts the view of a country parish church from behind a curtained window.
Commissioned by	Monica Capoferry
Client	Society for Promoting Christian Knowledge
Commissioned for	SPCK

 Sara Hayward
Gap

Self-Promotion

Medium	Mixed Media
Brief	A Collage to evoke transatlantic travel and a young person's first experiences of independance.

Victoria Rose

Business Strategy

Self-Promotion

Medium   Collage

Brief   Illustrate the front cover for a business strategy
leaflet for Grey London Advertising Agency.

Lars Rehnberg
Cixi, Empress Of China

Self-Promotion

Medium   Digital

Brief   The chinese dish Dim Sum was served for the first
time in the end of the 19th century to the empress
of China, Cixi.
Used as self promotion.

Lars Rehnberg
Starfish

Self-Promotion

Medium   Digital

Brief   Originally for OLF. The oil industry and the
environment. Unpublished and used as
self promotion.

Lars Rehnberg

Psychopath

Self-Promotion

Medium | Digital

Brief | Portrait of a psychopath. On the surface a very charming person, yet cold and scheming. Used as self promotion.

Ted Tuesday

This Virus

Self-Promotion

Medium | Mixed Media

Brief | Loose line drawing to illustrate song lyric "I don't know these strangers on my body". Feature a main figure in passive mode.

Commissioned by | E. Rex

Client | The Armed (Rock Group)

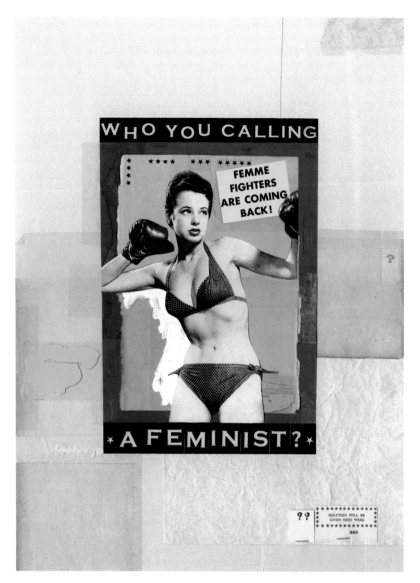

Caroline Tomlinson
Who You Calling A Feminist?

Self-Promotion

Medium   Collage

Brief   To accompany an article which attacks the
              stereotypical image of feminists.

Caroline Tomlinson
Catwalk

Self-Promotion

Medium   Collage

Brief   Article questioning what is more important, the
              garments or the celebrity model who wears them?

Michael Sheehy

La Passeggiata

Advertising

Medium	Mixed Media
Brief	An image to represent summer holidays: an evening stroll in an Italian town.
Commissioned by	Louisa St. Pierre/ Ben Cox
Client	Central Illustration Agency (CIA)

Michael Sheehy

Miss America

Self-Promotion

Medium	Mixed Media
Brief	The american way of life is a threat to the ecology and political stability of our planet.

Darren Hopes
Suburban Angel

Self-Promotion

Medium   Mixed Media
Brief   Keep the folio moving in new directions.

Darren Hopes
She Waits

Self-Promotion

Medium   Mixed Media
Brief   Self promotion aimed at the book publishing
                industry and so needed to contain a sense
                of narrative.

Paul Powis
We Three Kings

Design

Medium   Oils
Brief   One of a series of soft-focus drawings exploring the
                          way penguins walk.
Commissioned by   Glyn Washington

We three kings

Paul Powis

Legs

Self-Promotion

Medium   Mixed Media

Brief   To produce a concise summer fashion image using economy of line and colour.

195

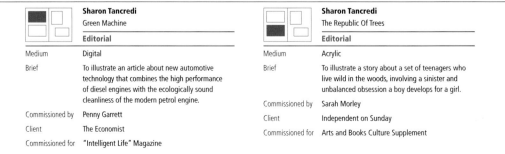

Sharon Tancredi
Green Machine

Editorial

Medium	Digital
Brief	To illustrate an article about new automotive technology that combines the high performance of diesel engines with the ecologically sound cleanliness of the modern petrol engine.
Commissioned by	Penny Garrett
Client	The Economist
Commissioned for	"Intelligent Life" Magazine

Sharon Tancredi
The Republic Of Trees

Editorial

Medium	Acrylic
Brief	To illustrate a story about a set of teenagers who live wild in the woods, involving a sinister and unbalanced obsession a boy develops for a girl.
Commissioned by	Sarah Morley
Client	Independent on Sunday
Commissioned for	Arts and Books Culture Supplement

Sharon Tancredi

Zodiac Totty

Self-Promotion

Medium	Digital
Brief	To design and illustrate a zodiac wheel poster for self promotional use.

Bob Venables

Determination

Advertising

Medium	Pencil
Brief	To produce an illustration that would give the effect of a chalk drawing on a pavement.
Commissioned by	Becky Foley
Client	Joshua Agency
Commissioned for	Cobra Beer

Amanda Addison
To Market......To Market

Books

Medium	Mixed Media
Brief	Produce a children's book which depicts the Norfolk broads and the history of the Norfolk Wherry Sail Craft.
Commissioned by	A.Addison
Client	Blacksail
Commissioned for	Creative Arts East on behalf of leader+

Orly Orbach
Who Killed Cock Robin

Books

Medium	Pen and Ink (line and wash)
Brief	Illustration based on explanations to the nursery rhyme. Inspired by mythological ideas about birds that transport human souls to the afterlife.
Client	Granta Publications
Commissioned for	Heavy Words Lightly Thrown

Paul Brown
Witness

Editorial

Medium	Mixed Media
Brief	'Safe' a radio play. A teenage witness puts her own life at risk by testifying and faces a life in police protection.
Client	Radio Times - BBC Worldwide
Commissioned for	Radio Times

Patrick Hat
Branching Out

Self-Promotion

Medium   Digital

Alison Barratt

Le Petit Larousse Illustré Cover

Books

Medium	Mixed Media
Brief	To illustrate and reinterpret the long standing brand-icon 'La Semeuse' (the seed-sower) for the cover of the 2006 edition to celebrate care and concern for the world we live in through ecology.
Commissioned by	Zaki Elia
Client	Z+Co Design Ltd.
Commissioned for	Larousse Publishing France

Shane McG
Evie's Mad Hair Day

Books

Medium   Digital

Brief   Cover art for 32 page picture book about a girl
             whose brilliant fantasy life means she's way too
             busy to brush her mad hair.

Commissioned by   Mike Jolly

Client   Templar Publishing

Paul Bowman
Mladic

Self-Promotion

Medium   Gouache

Brief   General Ratko Mladic led the forces that massacred
             seven to eight thousand Muslim men and boys in
             the UN declared 'safe' haven at Srebrenica, in 1995.

Trina Dalziel
Untitled

Editorial

Medium	Digital
Brief	One of three illustrations for an article on sextology.
Commissioned by	Will Fox
Client	She
Commissioned for	National Magazines

Julian Crouch
Mobile Phone

Self-Promotion

Medium	Digital

Nick Dewar

Senses

Editorial

Medium	Acrylic
Brief	To create an image to work with the coverline: Why you have 'at least' 21 senses.
Commissioned by	Alison Lawn
Client	New Scientist

Peter Horridge

Boston Beer Ship

Design

Medium	Digital
Brief	Re-Design and update in your calligraphic style an old drawing from company archives. To be used across a range of beer packaging.
Commissioned by	Robert Schuellein
Client	Boston Beer Co.

 Miriam Latimer
The Birds And The Bees

Self-Promotion

Medium   Collage

Brief   Speculative project for Editorial portfolio,
illustrating an article discussing relationships and
different forms of love.

 Jonathan Croft
Boxing

Editorial

Medium   Digital

Brief   To produce an illustration depicting a macho and
aggressive male-dominated sport.

Commissioned by   Catrin Hansmerten

Client   Kids Wear Magazine

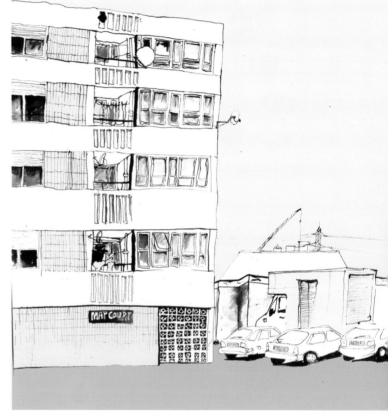

Simon Stephenson
The Seasons

Self-Promotion

Medium   Digital

Brief   Competition to illustrate the seasons in an original
            way to be used in a diary.

Clare Mallison
Maycourt

Self-Promotion

Medium   Mixed Media

Brief   Observational drawing on location in my
            home town.

Tina Ramsbottom
Iris

Design

Medium	Watercolour
Brief	Create large, bright energetic florals for use on posters to be sold as printed artwork for the home.
Commissioned by	Emily Holyfield
Client	The Art Group

Alex Williamson
Grey Area

Books

Medium	Digital
Brief	Book Cover for Will Self "Grey Area", book of short stories.
Commissioned by	Will Webb
Client	Bloomsbury Publishing
Commissioned for	Will Self "Grey Area"

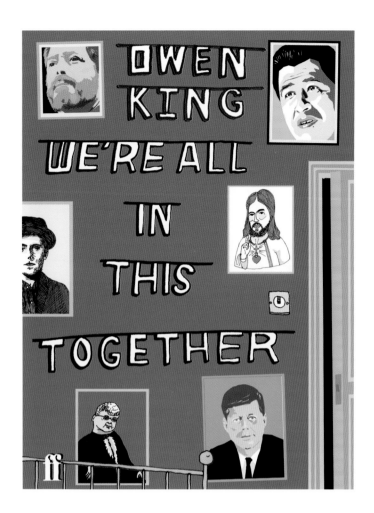

Harry Malt
Untitled

Books

Medium	Mixed Media
Brief	Produce a cover based on concerning characters.
Commissioned by	Donna Payne
Client	Faber and Faber

Lynda K. "Barley" Robinson
Cabaret Ladysinger

Advertising

Medium	Acrylic
Brief	Poster commissioned for Cabaret Recitals 2005 of 'Belter' cabaret songs by professional female 'Belter' vocaliste, and as programme cover. (Belter vocaliste - Lou Dietrich).
Commissioned by	Lou Live
Client	KKOS Music Pub
Commissioned for	Lou Live

Derek Brazell
Muslim Girl

Self-Promotion

Medium	Gouache and Pencil
Brief	To create an image of a muslim girl including elements of middle eastern art.

Jess Mikhail

Strawberry Jam

Self-Promotion

Medium   Mixed Media

Brief   Two adventurous bears stumble upon a scrumptious strawberry field.

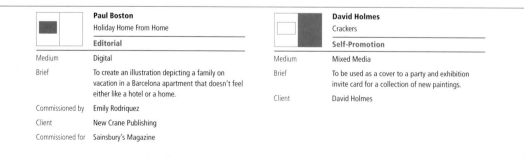

Paul Boston
Holiday Home From Home

Editorial

Medium	Digital
Brief	To create an illustration depicting a family on vacation in a Barcelona apartment that doesn't feel either like a hotel or a home.
Commissioned by	Emily Rodriquez
Client	New Crane Publishing
Commissioned for	Sainsbury's Magazine

David Holmes
Crackers

Self-Promotion

Medium	Mixed Media
Brief	To be used as a cover to a party and exhibition invite card for a collection of new paintings.
Client	David Holmes

Rebecca Bradley
Studio

Editorial

Medium	Mixed Media
Brief	Illustrate how movie studios can contain anything a filmmaker needs.
Commissioned by	Sarah Watson
Client	EMAP Media, Shots Magazine
Commissioned for	Shots 88

Stefan Isaacson
New Architecture By Tube, Bus And River

Self-Promotion

Medium	Screen Print
Brief	Competition brief to create artwork for use as part of a poster campaign to inform Londoners of modern architecture accessible via TFL networks.

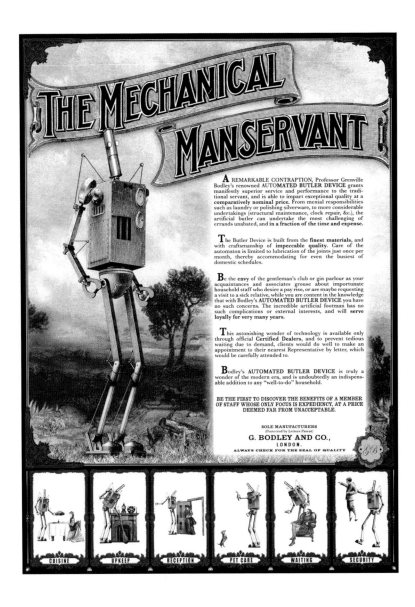

Peter Bowen

The Mechanical Manservant

Self-Promotion

Medium	Mixed Media
Brief	Antique print advertisement for a robot butler- state of the art technology (in the 19th century).

Derek Bacon

'Ing-ger-lund' (with apologies to Hogarth)

Advertising

Medium	Digital
Brief	First in a series of monthly promotional posters featuring individual illustrators from the agency. The image is a satirical take on Hogarth's 'Gin Lane'.
Commissioned by	Harry Lyon-Smith
Client	Illustration Ltd
Commissioned for	Monthly Promotional Poster

Tilly Northedge
AIDS In Africa

Design

Medium	Digital
Brief	Produce an illustration to explain the three possible outcomes for the AIDS epidemic in Africa.
Commissioned by	Julia Cleves
Client	UNAIDS
Commissioned for	Publication entitled 'AIDS In Africa: Three Scenarios To 2025'

Jacquie O'Neill
Spring Cocktail

Self-Promotion

Medium	Digital
Brief	For self promotion in a source book.

Lys Flowerday
Month Of March

Self-Promotion

Medium   Collage

Brief   Cover for Poetry and Literature magazine
           -March Issue.

Mayko Fry
The Haunted Sea

Self-Promotion

Medium   Mixed Media

Brief   The beginning of a ghost story for young readers.
           The sea was haunted by the dead spirits of the
           anicent samurai and their young lord.

Sarah Perkins
Making Light Work

Editorial

Medium	Mixed Media
Brief	To give a sense of the Australian outback, heat and isolation. A feeling of foreboding that leads to a mans disappearence.
Commissioned by	Denny Barnes
Client	Good Housekeeping

Kevin Hauff
Grouse Hunting In Scotland

Design

Medium	Digital
Brief	Illustration responding to an imaginary holiday activity for each member of the 741 Illustration collective for their summer brochure.
Commissioned by	Kirstie Talbot
Client	741 Illustration
Commissioned for	741 Illustration Agency Brochure

'Hypnotic, fast moving and intellectually challenging ... Staggeringly good'
DAILY MAIL

THE SOCIETY OF OTHERS
WILLIAM NICHOLSON

Andrew Pavitt
The Society Of Others

Books

Medium	Digital
Brief	Design a cover to suggest an environment of kafkaesque alienation.
Commissioned by	Gavin Morris
Client	Transworld Publishing

Jerry Hoare
Signalong

Design

Medium	Mixed Media and Pen
Brief	Signalong works with children and adults with communication difficulties, mostly caused by learning disability or autism. The image was for a calendar featuring 12 charities.
Commissioned by	Nick Belsen
Client	Origin Design
Commissioned for	Signalong

Anna - Louise Felstead MA(RCA)

Traders In Deutsche Bank

Design

Medium	Pen and Ink (line and wash)
Brief	Illustration for the Michael J. Lonsdale brochure describing the fact their company fitted the air conditioning for the London premises of Deutsche Bank.
Commissioned by	Michael Hoodless
Client	Michael J. Lonsdale

Leslie Carter

The Opiate Of The Masses

Self-Promotion

Medium	Digital
Brief	A personal response to the implicit hypocrisies of organised religion.

Patrick Regout

Trainee

Editorial

Medium	Mixed Media
Brief	For a Management Today magazine article about companies which take on students as trainees.
Commissioned by	Anne Braybon
Client	Management Today
Commissioned for	Management Today Magazine

David Broadbent

Sale

Self-Promotion

Medium	Acrylic
Brief	'Garage Sale' - to illustrate a desperate attempt to raise some funds for an unspecified purpose.

Paul Slater
What We Look For In A Prime Minister

Editorial

Medium	Acrylic
Brief	For an article about why we choose the Prime Ministers we do, and what we expect of them.
Commissioned by	Hugh Kyle
Client	Reader's Digest Magazine

John Miers
Don Quixote, Part 1, Book 3, Chapter 2

Self-Promotion

Medium	Mixed Media
Brief	Don Quixote and Soncho Panza ride towards an inn which Don Quixote mistakes for a castle.

Nicholas Rooke

Space Invasion

Self-Promotion

Medium   Digital

Brief   Speculative project for an article discussing the
              invasion of personal space, one of a series.

Imogen Slater

Love Lace

Self-Promotion

Medium   Digital

Brief   Greeting card design.

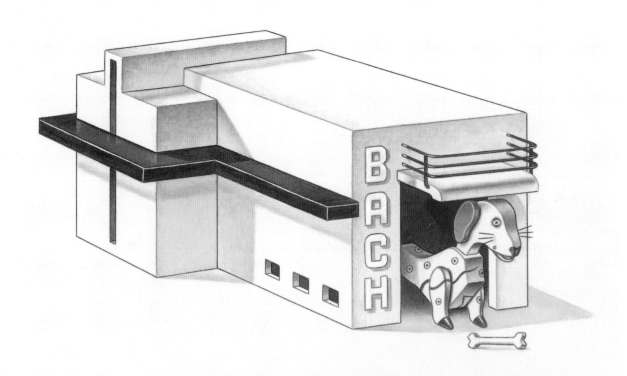

Tony McSweeney
Bauhaus

Books

Medium	Watercolour
Brief	To illustrate the new definition of Bauhaus i.e dog kennel for The Uxbridge English Dictionary. (Bach is a real german dog name).
Commissioned by	Tony Lyons
Client	Estuary English
Commissioned for	Harper Collins

Jason Ford
Edinburgh Festival

Editorial

Medium	Mixed Media
Brief	To produce a generic image that covered film, theatre, music, tattoo, books and fringe events at the Edinburgh Festival.
Commissioned by	Gavin Brammal
Client	The Guardian
Commissioned for	The Guardian Festival Guide

Jason Ford
Gardening

Self-Promotion

Medium	Mixed Media
Brief	One of a series of images looking at activities that people do in their spare time.

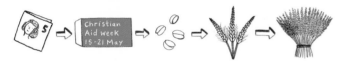

Harriet Russell
You Add, We Multiply

Advertising

Medium	Mixed Media
Brief	Illustrate a poster with the slogan 'You Add, We Multiply' to encourage people to donate money during Christian Aid Week.
Commissioned by	Dave Dye
Client	Campbell, Doyle, Dye
Commissioned for	Christian Aid

Harriet Russell
Jeeves And The Impending Doom

Books

Medium	Mixed Media
Brief	Design a cover illustration for the Penguin 70's series which should look unlike any other edition of Wodehouse.
Commissioned by	John Hamilton
Client	Penguin

Harriet Russell
Natural Flights Of The Human Mind

Books

Medium	Silkscreen
Brief	To produce a cover illustration with a lighthearted feel featuring a lighthouse and a large hand-lettered title.
Commissioned by	Alasdair Oliver
Client	Hodder

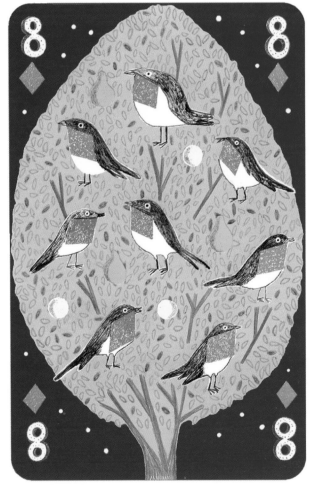

 Harriet Russell

Italian Terms

Self-Promotion

Medium   Mixed Media

Brief   Image for an exhibition of 'Postcard Confessionals'
             on the theme 'what did you do last summer?'.

Harriet Russell

8 Of Diamonds

Design

Medium   Mixed Media

Brief   To design a playing card with a Christmas theme.

Commissioned by   Lovisa Almgren

Client   Abbott Mead Vickers

Commissioned for   AMV BBDO

Andy Smith
Fatty Blew Away

Self-Promotion

Medium   Mixed Media
Brief   A page from self-published silkscreen-printed book
'Fattys Big Bubble.'

Andy Smith

Fatty Was Lost

Self-Promotion

Medium	Mixed Media
Brief	A page from self-published silkscreen-printed book 'Fattys Big Bubble.'

Kenneth Andersson
U.S. And Them

Self-Promotion

Medium   Mixed Media
Brief   For an exhibition inspired by a trip to see a relative
             in Austin, Nevada.

Kenneth Andersson
Bar

Self-Promotion

Medium   Mixed Media
Brief   For an exhibition inspired by a trip to see a relative
             in Austin, Nevada.

Kenneth Andersson

Flowers

Self-Promotion

Medium	Mixed Media
Brief	Self-promotional postcard, one of a set of four.

Kenneth Andersson

Miau!

Editorial

Medium	Mixed Media
Brief	For an article about sounds in television.
Client	Televisual Magazine

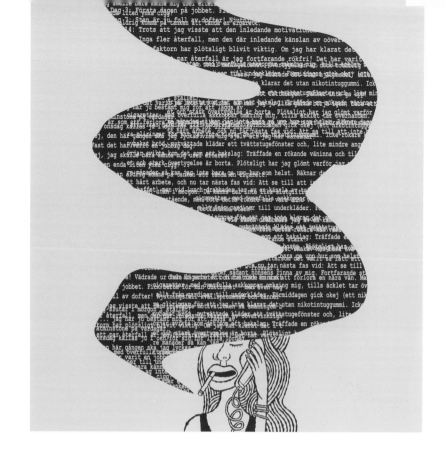

Kenneth Andersson
Gun Girl

Self-Promotion

Medium   Mixed Media

Brief   For an exhibition inspired by a trip to see a relative
in Austin, Nevada.

Kenneth Andersson
Smoke

Self-Promotion

Medium   Mixed Media

Brief   For an article about a special telephone line for
people who want to stop smoking.

Kenneth Andersson
The Collector

Self-Promotion

Medium   Mixed Media

Brief   For an article about the connection between
collecting things and science.

The Collector

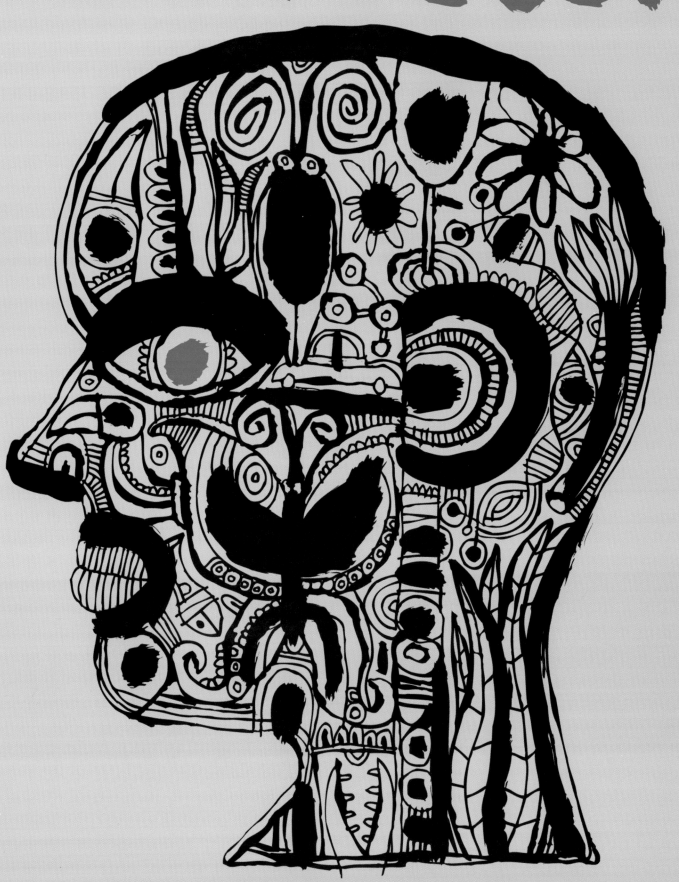

'When I first went to art school there were almost no illustration courses. Now there are lots, and millions of illustrators. It is harder than it has ever been to get recognised. This makes it really important to develop your own style – whatever that is [it's whatever feels comfortable] because, in the end, the quality that shines through and makes one piece of artwork preferable and more interesting than another – is honesty.'

Emma Chichester Clarke

New Talent

'I've been enjoying the return of drawing to contemporary art and the crossover between the two realms in recent years. From the contrived naivety popularised by David Shrigley, through the new imagists such as Chad McCail, to the mannered pencil sketches of Charles Avery, fine artists have borrowed from and fed into illustration not merely stylistically, but in a way that promotes illustrators as authors of an alternative form of storytelling. Whether its serialised in the chapbooks of the Cabanon Press or dangling from bulldog clips at the Glasgow Drawing Club, a wry, narrative and enigmatic 'penmanship' is enjoying welcome prominence.'

Cavan Convery

Emma Chichester Clark
Illustrator

Emma Chichester Clark studied at Chelsea School of Art and the Royal College of Art. She worked as a freelance illustrator for magazines and advertising agencies and illustrated over a hundred book covers. Since then she has worked as a childrens' book illustrator and author. Her books include the Blue Kangaroo series and recently, two new characters, Melrose and Croc.

Cavan Convery
Illustrator and Art Director, Product Magazine, Edinburgh

Cavan has worked as a designer and illustrator for over 10 years. Designing for a wide variety of media from exhibitions to magazines, and illustrating in a broad range of styles from cartoon to medical. His present clients include the National Galleries of Scotland and Edinburgh International Science Festival. He is currently working on several animations illustrating communication in sea mammals.
Cavan is also a practicing artist working in new media. His art works have featured in group shows at the Baltic, CCA and Stills gallery in Edinburgh.

Patrick Coyne
Editor/Designer, Communications Arts Magazine, California

Patrick Coyne is editor and designer of Communication Arts magazine, the world's largest trade journal on visual communications. In addition to determining the layout and content of the magazine, Mr. Coyne writes feature stories and the editor's column.

Sara Fanelli
Illustrator

Sara Fanelli was born in Florence, Italy. She came to London to study art and has been working here as a freelance illustrator ever since she graduated from the Royal College of Art in 1995. Her clients include The New Yorker, The New York Times, Penguin Books, The Tate, Ron Arad, BBC Worldwide and The Royal Mail. She is also well known for her children's books (including Dear Diary, First Flight, Mythological Monsters and Pinocchio) for which she has won several international awards.

Nick Schon
Illustrator and Freelance Art Director

Nick started illustrating 15 years ago when he was an art director working for Saatchi and Saatchi. His son George had a minor bicycle prang and he turned the incident into a story which eventually got him his first commission. He has worked for Penguin, Harper Collins, Pearson, OUP, CUP, Reed, Ginn and a long list of other publishers since then.

'As illustration is increasingly being squeezed by tighter budgets and deadlines, I expect to see more self-initiated projects from these truly talented creative communicators.'
Patrick Coyne

233

"Who killed Cock Robin?"

1. Winning illustration
2. A Real Crow - Sketch
3. 'Beaky' the Stork - Sketch
4. My Gangster Friends - Sketch
5. First Sketch

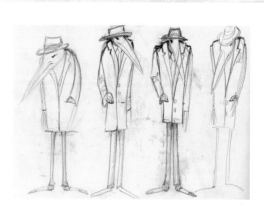

'Well?,
OK, who made the plans for the
Great Cheese Robbery?'

Slight shuffle of feet and
gaze of some gangsters.
*owl "The hoot"
raises his wing to confess.
Specific lighting casting shadows on the
measurement wall behind.

GOLD

Susan Webber

Who Made The Plans?

University of West of England

Medium	Acrylic
Brief	A student project to produce a children's book. I took "Who killed cock Robin" and set it in gangster birdland New York.
Course Leader	Ian McCullough
Course	BA (Hons) Illustration

Susan Webber studied at U.W.E., the University of the West of England, Bristol, graduating in 2005 with a BA (hons) in illustration. She loved every minute and subject, creating 3D objects, pop-ups, studying word and image, image and observation, as 'artist in residence' to her final study of children's book illustration. Susan won a "highly commended" in the Macmillan prize 2005 for 'Who killed Cock Robin?'

Susan loves simple pencil line and painting with acrylic. In order for her paintings to have detail she gathers as much information as possible to build a believable other world. Her favorite subjects are flora and fauna.

Over the years, Susan has painted stage scenery, pet portraits, designed and decorated wooden toys and many other weird and wonderful things.

She loves travel, photography, penguins and Robin Hood.

235

SILVER

Tom Burns

Crossing Paths

Kingston University

Medium	Mixed Media
Brief	One of a series of illustrations for articles depicting personal accounts of people's lives, this image focuses on a 'chance meeting'.
Course Leader	Robin Harris
Course	MA Illustration and Animation

Tom Burns graduated from Exeter School of Art in 2001. From there he moved abroad

working, travelling and living in Europe, South America, Australasia and South East Asia for just under two years. He documented this period in time through drawing and photography, and it gave significant influence to his use of colour and composition within his illustration work.

The MA at Kingston University brought Tom to London and gave him the time to develop a personal visual language and style within the illustration discipline.

BRONZE

Martyn Shouler

Warlord

University of Luton

Medium	Mixed Media
Brief	One of a series of provocative quotes from the bible, which were included in a book I produced for my major project.
Course Leader	Ed D'Souza
Course	BA (Hons) Graphic Design

Martyn Shouler was born in Bedford (UK) in 1961. After leaving school with aspirations of creativity and a handful of worthless qualifications he decided to pursue a career in nursing, firstly in a grand old Victorian asylum and then at a general hospital where he encountered the truly psychotic, most of them in upper management.

After leaving the NHS Martyn eventually worked his way into magazine and brochure production: artworking, designing and setting type. In 2002, circumstances prompted him to take a degree in graphic design at The University of Luton, which, he claims, was probably the best decision he has ever made.

Martyn started side-stepping grids, became obsessed with mess-making and started drawing again.

He is currently studying an MA in Communication Design at Central Saint Martins and has no plans to get any older.

 Martyn Shouler
Open Spaces

University of Luton

Medium   Mixed Media

Brief   Poster Campaign to create awareness of London's
                open spaces accessible by public transport.

Course Leader   Ed D'Souza

Course   BA (Hons) Graphic Design

 Nahoshi Tanaka
Oberon Books Illustration Awards 2005

Royal College of Art

Medium   Pencil

Brief   Poster for Oberon Books Illustration Awards
                competition which is sponsored by the
                communication department at the Royal College
                of Art.

Course Leader   Dan Fern

Course   Communication Art and Design

David Gibson
Sleep Is Death Lite

University College Falmouth

Medium	Digital
Brief	Illustrate an article describing one man's fear of going to sleep.
Course Leader	Alan Male
Course	Illustration

David Gibson
Price Of Fish

University College Falmouth

Medium	Digital
Brief	Illustrate an article on the future prices of cod in this country.
Course Leader	Alan Male
Course	Illustration

Lisa Linnea
Adventures At Sea

Kingston University

Medium	Watercolour
Brief	Create an image to be used as a poster for a concert for children entitled 'Adventures at Sea', the title needs to be in the image.
Course Leader	Brian Love and Jake Abrams
Course	BA Illustration

Lisa Linnea
Star-stealing Raindeer

Kingston University

Medium	Watercolour
Brief	A character for own story about a little girl and a mysterious Raindeer...
Course Leader	Brian Love and Jake Abrams
Course	BA Illustration

Lisa Linnea
Maria Sibylla Merians Inspiration

Kingston University

Medium	Watercolour
Brief	Create a series of images portraying someones collection.
Course Leader	Brian Love and Jake Abrams
Course	BA Illustration

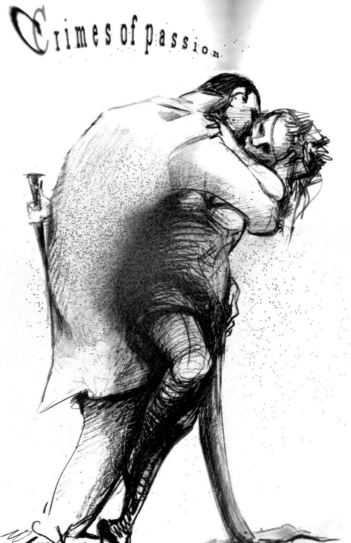

Rachel Swirles
Dolor

University of Lincoln

Medium	Acrylic
Brief	Produce a personal response to Roethke's poem "Dolor".
Course Leader	Howard Pemberton
Course	BA (Hons) Illustration

Vuokko Keiski
Crimes Of Passion

University of West of England

Medium	Mixed Media
Brief	Depict cold blooded passion.
Course Leader	Ian McCullough
Course	BA (Hons) Illustration

Matt Broersma
Haymarket Martyrs

Birmingham Institute of Art and Design/ UCE

Medium	Mixed Media
Brief	Illustrate an event in progressive history, The Haymarket Affair. Illustration is for May Day in a calendar for ATTAC, a progressive organisation.
Course Leader	Andrew Kulman
Course	MA Visual Communication

Ayako Morisawa

Bonsai

University College Falmouth

Medium	Mixed Media
Brief	I created this image based on a bonsai tree. Terminology Ishi Seki: Planted on rock with decorative style.
Course Leader	Alan Male
Course	BA (Hons) Illustration

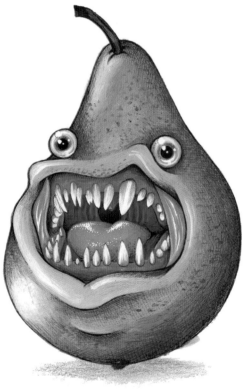

Adam Fisher

Creation Stories - Ainu

University of Wales Institute, Cardiff

Medium	Mixed Media
Brief	To illustrate some of the worlds most facinating and bizarre creation tales for an illustrated book, in this instance the image is of Ainu, an early Japanese tale.
Course Leader	Kevin Edge
Course	Graphic Communication

Adam Fisher

Creation Stories - Aboriginal

University of Wales Institute, Cardiff

Medium	Acrylic
Brief	To illustrate some of the worlds most facinating and bizarre creation tales for an illustrated book, in this instance the image is of an early Aboriginal tale.
Course Leader	Kevin Edge
Course	Graphic Communication

Adam Fisher

Pear

University of Wales Institute, Cardiff

Medium	Acrylic
Brief	To produce an image for an article discussing GM foods.
Course Leader	Kevin Edge
Course	Graphic Communication

Adam Fisher

Creation Stories - Norse

University of Wales Institute, Cardiff

Adam Fisher

Death Of A Mouse

University of Wales Institute, Cardiff

Ridade Al - Daghestani
Breathe

Duncan of Jordanstone College of Art and Design

Medium	Manipulation and Digital Photography
Brief	Visual display of the Circassian culture within a contemporary ethos. Highlighting dance, as a way to show implicit and explicit elements of nobility and nature.
Course Leader	Marlene Ivey and Georgina Follett
Course	Masters of Design (MDes) (specialising in Illustration)

Ridade Al - Daghestani
My Soul

Duncan of Jordanstone College of Art and Design

Medium	Digital
Brief	Visual display of the Circassian culture within a contemporary ethos. Highlighting the relationship between male and female, emulating love, spirituality, and harmony with the Caucasus mountains.
Course Leader	Marlene Ivey and Georgina Follett
Course	Masters of Design (MDes) (specialising in Illustration)

Ridade Al - Daghestani
Spirit Of The Dancer

Duncan of Jordanstone College of Art and Design

Medium	Digital
Brief	Visual display of the Circassian culture within a contemporary ethos. Highlighting dance, as a way to show implicit and explicit elements of nobility and nature.
Course Leader	Marlene Ivey and Georgina Follett
Course	Masters of Design (MDes) (specialising in Illustration)

wolfy had never seen a strawberry in his life. The strawberry looked delicious and wolfy ate it. He magically turned into a strawberry wolfy.

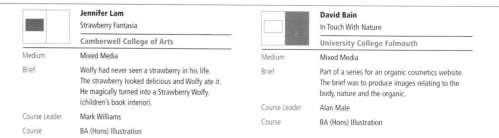

	Jennifer Lam			**David Bain**
	Strawberry Fantasia			In Touch With Nature
	Camberwell College of Arts			**University College Falmouth**
Medium	Mixed Media		Medium	Mixed Media
Brief	Wolfy had never seen a strawberry in his life. The strawberry looked delicious and Wolfy ate it. He magically turned into a Strawberry Wolfy. (children's book interior).		Brief	Part of a series for an organic cosmetics website. The brief was to produce images relating to the body, nature and the organic.
Course Leader	Mark Williams		Course Leader	Alan Male
Course	BA (Hons) Illustration		Course	BA (Hons) Illustration

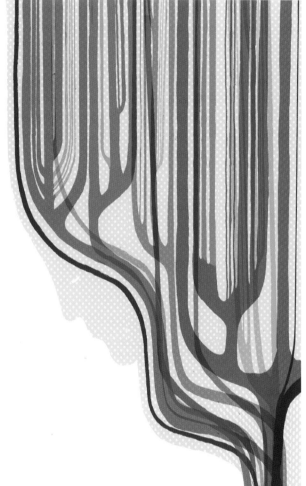

Alice Stevenson
The Mystery

University of Brighton

Medium	Mixed Media
Brief	An image in response to the quote by Albert Einstein: "The most beautiful thing we can ever experience is the mystery, it is the source of all true art and science".
Course Leader	Lawrence Zeegen
Course	BA (Hons) Illustration

Emily Warren
Beauty

Central St. Martins

Medium	Mixed Media
Brief	"Beauty", a self-initiated project to produce a series of portraits.
Course Leader	Andrew Foster
Course	MA Illustration

Yvonne Lee
Meursault's View

University Of Derby

Medium	Mixed Media
Brief	From a series of images for the book 'The Outsider', by Albert Camus. This image is highlighting Meursault's psychological freedom and view of society.
Course Leader	Jane Stanton
Course	BA (Hons) Illustration

Yvonne Lee

Meursault Captured

University Of Derby

Medium	Mixed Media
Brief	From a series of images for the book, 'The Outsider' by Albert Camus, exploring society's mask of conventions and beliefs in context of the story.
Course Leader	Jane Stanton
Course	BA (Hons) Illustration

Elaine Kelso
Daddy's Boy

University of Hertfordshire

Medium	Mixed Media
Brief	An illustrative interpretation of jealousy based on the biblical story 'Joseph', when his brothers plot to kill him. (Forms part of a collectors type journal).
Course Leader	Martin Schooley
Course	BA(Hons) Graphic Design and Illustration

253

Jay Taylor
Old Age

University Of Central Lancashire

Medium   Mixed Media

Brief   Self initiated project where I could only use material
            which I came across at the scene of the initial
            drawing, which was later put together on computer.

Course Leader   Steve Wilkin

Course   BA (Hons) Illustration

Jay Taylor
How To Garden

University Of Central Lancashire

Medium   Mixed Media

Brief   Image to support an article on how to garden.

Course Leader   Steve Wilkin

Course   BA (Hons) Illustration

Images 30 **New Talent**

Susan Webber
I Said The Owl

University of the West of England

Medium	Acrylic
Brief	A student project to produce a children's book. I took 'Who killed cock Robin' and set it in 1920s gangster birdland New York.
Course Leader	Ian McCullough
Course	BA (Hons) Illustration

Susan Webber
The Tin Soldier And The Goblin

University of the West of England

Medium	Acrylic
Brief	To produce a set of colourful images for the story 'The Steadfast Tin Soldier'. This one is an atmospheric midnight toy scene.
Course Leader	Ian McCullough
Course	BA (Hons) Illustration

Luke Knight
The Beast Inside

University of the West of England

Medium	Mixed Media
Brief	Produce a book cover illustration for William Golding's 'The Lord of the Flies'.
Course Leader	Ian McCullough
Course	BA (Hons) Illustration

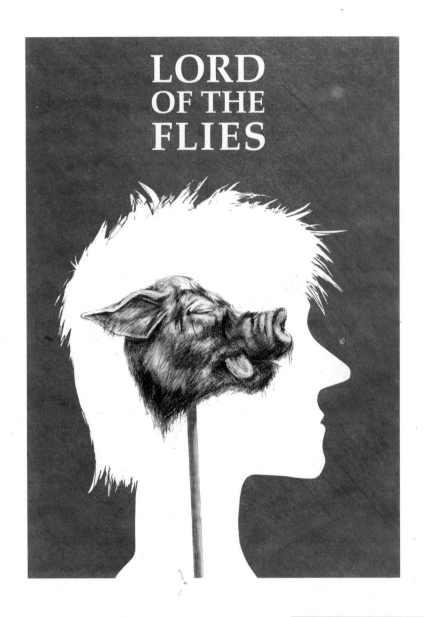

LORD
OF THE
FLIES

Luke Knight

Megalomania

University of the West of England

Medium	Mixed Media
Brief	One of a series of images illustrating psychological traits.
Course Leader	Ian McCullough
Course	BA (Hons) Illustration

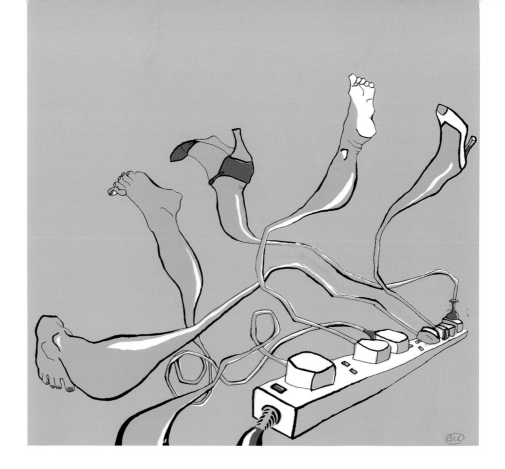

Sarah Coulston
Electric Heels

Birmingham Institute of Art & Design, UCE

Medium	Silkscreen
Brief	Music promotion; the cover for a CD of contemporary music. It must represent music in the 21st century.
Course Leader	George Hart
Course	BA (Hons) Illustration

Gemma Robinson
Bird Flu

Loughborough University

Medium	Mixed Media
Brief	An illustration to accompany an article about the possibility of a bird flu virus spreading to humans.
Course Leader	Andrew Selby
Course	BA (Hons) Illustration

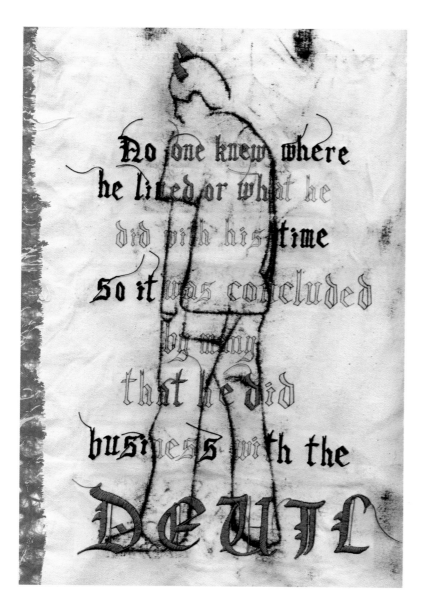

No one knew where he lived or what he did with his time

So it was concluded by many that he did

business with the

DEUTL

Faye Tabone

A Man Called Sedgewick

Surrey Institute of Art and Design

Medium	Mixed Media
Brief	Create illustrations and depict part of/all of the story based on the story "The Legendary Sledgewick" by Ben Okri.
Course Leader	Susanna Edwards
Course	BA Graphic Communication

Kath Allsopp

Into The Wood

Brighton University

Medium	Mixed Media
Brief	From a book using fairy tale symbolism to explore ideas about growing up.
Course Leader	George Hardie
Course	MA Sequential Design/Illustration

and the great sea monsters...

Rebecca Canavan
Rising Moon

Edinburgh College of Art

Medium	Mixed Media
Brief	To produce an atmospheric illustration based on a haiku about a toad and the moon.
Course Leader	Jonathan Gibbs
Course	Master of Design (Illustration)

Rebecca Canavan
Sea Monsters

Edinburgh College of Art

Medium	Mixed Media
Brief	Double page spread for a children's book about the creation of all living things. An emphasis is put on depth and atmosphere.
Course Leader	Jonathan Gibbs
Course	Master of Design (Illustration)

Irfana Biviji
All Looks The Same?

University College Falmouth

Medium	Marker Pen
Brief	A hypothetical book jacket on Industrial Working Class in Bombay.
Course Leader	Alan Male
Course	Illustration

Richard Keith Liptrot
US Soldier

University of Central Lancashire

Medium	Mixed Media
Brief	Produce an image for an article advertising an exhibition about president Bush and the war in Iraq to be held in Manchester, "The Basement".
Course Leader	Steve Wilkin
Course	Illustration

Paula Bowles
Plane Mobile

University College Falmouth

Medium	Digital
Brief	Editorial illustration for article "one in twelve plane crashes are caused by pilots falling asleep".
Course Leader	Alan Male
Course	BA (hons) Illustration

Jemma Claire Robinson
London 2012?

Loughborough University

Medium	Digital
Brief	Illustrate the potential negative impact on London residents of the London 2012 Olympics, and explore the effect it will have on the city.
Course Leader	Andrew Selby
Course	BA (Hons) Illustration

Andy Hixon
Nine To Five

Stockport College of Higher Education

Medium	Mixed Media
Brief	For an article 'My nine to five job is turning me into a machine'.
Course Leader	Gary Spicer
Course	BA (Hons) Illustration

Andy Hixon
Tsunami Aid

Stockport College of Higher Education

Medium	Mixed Media
Brief	Create an image for editorial to show how 'tsunami aid' is needed on an epic scale.
Course Leader	Gary Spicer
Course	BA (Hons) Illustration

Benedict Siddle
Pull My Daisy

Kent Institute of Art and Design

Medium   Screen Print
Brief   Illustrate the poem 'Pull My Daisy'
                by Allen Ginsberg.
Course Leader   Neil Breeden
Course   BA (Hons) Illustration

Benedict Siddle
Kiss Ass

Kent Institute of Art and Design

Medium   Screen Print
Brief   Illustrate the poem 'Kiss Ass' by Allen Ginsberg.
Course Leader   Neil Breeden
Course   BA (Hons) Illustration

But the Flying-Fishes laughed at her because she has a problem:

She's got no wings...

no wings

You see?
That's what I told you

Benedict Siddle
Little Red Riding Hood

Kent Institute of Art and Design

Medium	Mixed Media
Brief	Create a double page spread based on the fairytale 'Little Red Riding Hood'.
Course Leader	Neil Breeden
Course	BA (Hons) Illustration

Dimitri Minot
Sardine

Swindon College

Medium	Digital
Brief	Create a childrens story and develop a number of pages/illustrations to show its development.
Course Leader	Graham Smith
Course	HND Illustration

 Rachel Horton
Dinner Lady

Loughborough University

Medium	Mixed Media
Brief	Image from editorial series based on the issue of unhealthy school dinners. This piece - the menacing pudding server.
Course Leader	Andrew Selby
Course	BA (Hons) Illustration

 Yiqiao Jiang
Forest

Camberwell College of Art

Medium	Mixed Media
Brief	Image taken from a magazine project, idea based on the relationship between human and nature.
Course Leader	Mark Williams
Course	BA (Hons) Illustration

 Richard Oliver
Thought Police

Herefordshire College Of Art And Design

Medium	Digital
Brief	Create a poster campaign advertising a re-publication of George Orwell's 'Nineteen- Eighty-Four'.
Course Leader	Emily Mitchell
Course	BA (Hons) Illustration

Caroline Crampton
Sore Eyes

Cambridge School of Art (ARU)

Medium	Mixed Media
Brief	Editorial Illustration for health column-effect of chlorine in swimming pools.
Course Leader	Martin Salisbury
Course	BA (Hons) Illustration

Caroline Crampton
Weekend Day

Cambridge School of Art (ARU)

Medium	Mixed Media
Brief	Illustration in 40 day food diary.
Course Leader	Martin Salisbury
Course	BA (Hons) Illustration

Joe Frost

Hansel And Gretel

Loughborough University

Medium	Collage
Brief	To rework a classic fairytale in a contemporary style.
Course Leader	Andrew Selby
Course	BA (Hons) Illustration

Liza Seel

That Yellow Dress

Birmingham Institute of Arts & Design, UCE

Medium	Mixed Media
Brief	Create suggestive narratives, exploring the motivations and consequences towards our fashion conscious society, using symbolic birds, tone and atmosphere to depict such a theme.
Course Leader	George Hart
Course	BA (Hons) Visual Communication/Illustration

Sarah Hanson
New Architecture By Tube, Bus And River

University Of Hertfordshire

Medium	Collage
Brief	To produce artwork, suitable for use as a poster for Transport for London designed to inform all Londoners of the wide variety of modern architecture accessible by Tfl networks.
Course Leader	Martin Schooley
Course	(BA Hons) Graphic Design and Illustration

Sarah Hanson
People vs. Cars

University Of Hertfordshire

Medium	Mixed Media
Brief	To produce a series of images illustrating alternative aspects of culture for a book called "A Day Trip To Rome". This is one in the series and was inspired by drivers attitudes towards pedestrians.
Course Leader	Martin Schooley
Course	(BA Hons) Graphic Design and Illustration

Louise Tyers
Mauve Monsters

University College Falmouth

Medium	Mixed Media
Brief	To create a fun and exciting image to appeal to the child readers of a poetry anthology.
Course Leader	Alan Male
Course	BA (Hons) Illustration

Images 30 **New Talent**

Simon Clark

The City

The Arts Institute at Bournemouth

Medium	Digital
Brief	A page from a graphic novel dealing with a modern society, focusing on the desensitisation one encounters from living in a city.
Course Leader	Amanda Evans
Course	BA (Hons) Illustration

Laure Fournier

African Proverbs

Swindon College

Medium	Mixed Media
Brief	Create a number of images showing a range of african proverbs.
Course Leader	Graham Smith
Course	HND Illustration

Lauren Bishop

My Being Well

University College Falmouth

Medium	Mixed Media
Brief	Create an image for use on a website selling organic beauty products. Image must reflect themes: Nature and beauty.
Course Leader	Alan Male
Course	BA (Hons) Illustration

"Quand la mémoire va chercher le bois mort,

elle ramène le fagot qui lui plaît."

"Dieu n'a fait qu'ébaucher l'Homme,

c'est sur Terre

que chacun se crée."

(proverbe africain)

Alice Wood
See You Soon

Cambridge School of Art (ARU)

Medium	Etching and Watercolour
Brief	To write and illustrate a picture book, based on a drawing project at the Little Angel Puppet Theatre in London.
Course Leader	Martin Salisbury
Course	MA Children's Book Illustration

Emily Jepps
Butterfly

Kent Institute of Art and Design

Medium	Mixed Media
Brief	Make a contemporary children's book illustrating the victorian poem 'The Butterfly's Ball and the Grasshopper's Feast' by William Roscoe.
Course Leader	Neil Breeden
Course	BA (Hons) Illustration

Dan Bramall
The Possibilities Of Not Being You

Kingston University

Medium	Mixed Media
Brief	Poster promoting MA book based on research exploring the subjects of identity, imposture and disguise.
Course Leader	Robin Harris
Course	MA Illustration

Dan Bramall
Bank Robber

Kingston University

Medium	Mixed Media
Brief	Spread taken from "The Possibilities of Not Being You".
Course Leader	Robin Harris
Course	MA Illustration

Harvey
How To... Climb Trees

University of Central Lancashire

Medium	Print / Mixed Media
Brief	A personal project to illustrate a newspaper article entitled 'How to… climb trees'.
Course Leader	Steve Wilkin
Course	BA (Hons) Illustration

Harvey
Cloud Seeding

University of Central Lancashire

Medium	Print / Mixed Media
Brief	A personal project to illustrate a magazine article relating to the man-made ways to encourage rain.
Course Leader	Steve Wilkin
Course	BA (Hons) Illustration

 Salvatore Rubbino

New York Taxis

Royal College of Art

Medium	Mixed Media
Brief	From a book tracing a journey through the Big Apple at street level exploring the drama of city life.
Course Leader	Dan Fern
Course	MA Communication Art and Design

 Claire Failes

Piggy Back

University of West of England

Medium	Acrylic
Brief	Self initated project, turning the landscape into a narrative.
Course Leader	Ian McCullough
Course	BA (Hons) Illustration

Images 30 **New Talent**

 Thomas Dowse
Shipwright's Avenue

Kent Institute of Art & Design

Medium	**Mixed Media**
Brief	Illustration from an artists book set in Chatham, Kent called 'The Ivory Tower', that depicted the reality of the recent 'chav' phenomenon.
Course Leader	**Neil Breeden**
Course	BA (Hons) Illustration

Amy Rogers
Yellow Bed

Cambridge School of Art (ARU)

Medium	Oils
Brief	Contemplative self-portrait, capturing the moment between waking and dreaming.
Course Leader	Martin Salisbury
Course	BA (Hons) Illustration

AOI **Membership Benefits**

The Association of Illustrators provides a voice for professional illustrators and by weight of numbers and expertise is able to enforce the rights of freelance illustrators at every stage of their careers.

Membership of the AOI is open to all professional illustrators, illustration students, agents, lecturers and illustration clients.

All categories of membership receive the following benefits:
- Free distribution of Varoom – the journal of illustration and made images, an 84-page magazine celebrating the best in contemporary visual culture
- Free distribution of AOI info poster, UP! – the newsletter to hang on your wall!
- Discounted rates for Images – competition entries, hanging fees and annual pages
- Contact details on AOI database for enquiries from clients
- Discounts on art materials
- Large discounts on AOI events and publications

In addition, we provide the following services for particular types of membership:

Full Membership

This category is for professional illustrators who have had a minimum of three works commissioned in the previous 12 months prior to application and accept the AOI code of conduct:
- Dedicated phone line for legal and pricing advice
- Substantial discount on portfolio surgeries with a professional consultant
- Business advice – an hour's free consultation with a chartered accountant on accounts, bookkeeping, National Insurance, VAT and tax
- Only full members are entitled to use the affix 'Mem AOI'
- Discounted Web promotion opportunities through AOI portfolios

Associate Membership

The benefits are the same as those for full membership but this category is designed to assist illustrators starting out in the industry or those who are returning to a career in illustration. This allows the same benefits as full membership (without the prefix 'Mem AOI') and is reviewed regularly.

Student Membership

This service is for students on full-time illustration or related courses:
- Experts' advice on entering the profession
- Substantial discount on portfolio surgeries with a professional consultant
- Further discounts on AOI events, publications and competition entry
- Discounted Web promotion opportunities through AOI portfolios

Corporate Membership

This service is for agents and clients from the illustration industry who adhere to the AOI code of practice.
Further benefits:
- Free copy of the Images illustration annual
- All corporate members' staff and member agent represented illustrators will receive discounts on events, Images competition and AOI publications

College Membership

College membership entitles the college to the following benefits:
- Large discounts on AOI events and publications
- Link to college web page from AOI site
- Free copy of the Images illustration annual
- The right to use the AOI member logo on publicity
- Discounted Web promotion opportunities through AOI degree shows

Additional options (at extra cost) include:
- Portfolio consultations for groups or individual students
- Career Advice Lecture covering self-promotion, copyright, pricing, licencing, the work of the AOI, and the speaker's working practice etc.
- Bulk publication orders of Survive – Essential information for students on starting out and/or Rights – covering aspects of the law likely to affect illustrators
- Degree show presence on AOI website – portfolio option to maximise your students exposure.

For an application form and cost details please contact

Association of Illustrators
2nd Floor, Back Building
London EC2A 3AT
Tel: +44 (0) 20 7613 4328
Fax: +44 (0) 20 7613 4417

E-mail: info@theaoi.com
Website: www.theaoi.com

AOI **Resources**

Publications

Survive – The Illustrator's Guide to a Professional Career

Published by the AOI and revised in 2001, Survive is the only comprehensive and in-depth guide to illustration as a professional career. Established illustrators, agents, clients and a range of other professionals have contributed to this fourth edition. Each area of the profession including portfolio presentation, self-promotion and copyright issues are looked at in detail. The wealth of information in Survive makes it absolutely indispensable to the newcomer and also has much to offer the more experienced illustrator.

Rights – The Illustrator's Guide to Professional Practice

Rights is an all inclusive guide to aspects of the law specifically related to illustration. It includes information about copyright, contracts, book publishing agreements, agency agreements, how to seek legal advice, how to calculate fees and guidance on how to write a licence.

Rights is the result of a number of years research. It has been approved by solicitors and contains the most detailed and accurate model terms and conditions available for use by illustrators or clients.

Report on illustration fees and standards of pricing

In 2005, the AOI published a report entitled 'Illustration Fees and Standards of Pricing'. This publication is compiled from existing AOI data, general survey results and contributions from agents, art buyers and selected working professionals.

Research suggests that the decline of fees and/or commission charges for illustrations in recent years has resulted in many business failures. Properly researched costing and pricing structures is a central plank in maintaining business viability. Illustrators should consider the true cost of their services when determining rates. AOI hopes that this report will encourage both illustrators and commissioners to create awareness of the importance of carefully considered pricing.

Client directories

The Publishing Directory lists about 180 and the Editorial Directory more than 300 illustration clients with full contact details; the Advertising Directory holds details of over 200 advertising agencies who commission illustration – providing an invaluable source of information for all practitioners. Each directory includes notes of what kind of illustration is published by the client and we update and add contact details to each list every year.

To order publications, please send a cheque, made payable to the Association of Illustrators, clearly stating your contact details and which publications you would like to purchase to:

AOI Publications, 2nd Floor, Back Building, 150 Curtain Road, London, EC2A 3AT

For payment by Visa, Mastercard or Maestro, please call +44 (0)20 7613 4328 or subscribe/order online: www.theaoi.com/publications

Information

Great new membership poster, UP!

UP issues all regular AOI news, events and industry related information previously published in the discontinued magazine, The Journal.

UP is a collectible item each time featuring another unique image-maker. UP not only looks good on your walls but also represents the AOI's commitment to contemporary illustration and our ongoing success in promoting it. Award winning design duo Non-Format, until recently designers of The Wire magazine, have created the contemporary eye-catching layout.

UP is distributed four times a year to AOI members.

Keep up to date with Despatch online newsletter

Published bimonthly, Despatch brings you the latest industry news, AOI events information, campaigns, initiatives and reviews of relevant exhibitions and publications. To subscribe, visit www.theaoi.com/submissions

www.theaoi.com – illustration resources for commissioners and practitioners

Visit the AOI's website for details of the Association's activities, including past and current Despatch newsletter, information on our new magazine, Varoom – the journal of illustration and made images, details of forthcoming events and campaigns, the AOI's history, and to order publications, book tickets and display and browse online portfolios.

Varoom – the journal of illustration and made images

What is the role of illustration and the made image in contemporary society?
Why do the most fashionable brands commission illustration?
Where can you see the most compelling imagery?

Varoom features interviews with leading illustrators and image-makers and explores the attitude behind their designs. The magazine will look at influential movements in illustration and why they have succeeded in making a statement. An archive section will concentrate on different figures and schools of illustration, while the new voices section will showcase emerging talent.

Regular features from acclaimed design critics and practitioners such as Steven Heller will discuss contemporary illustration in its wider context and from different, even contentious, perspectives. Varoom will also review noteworthy exhibitions, events and publications.

Published three times a year, 84 pages, ISSN 1750-483X, available in specialist bookshops and assorted news stand in the UK, Europe, USA and Canada, free to members.

To subscribe, please visit our website www.theaoi.com, email subscribe@varoom-mag.com or call +44 (0) 20 7613 4328.

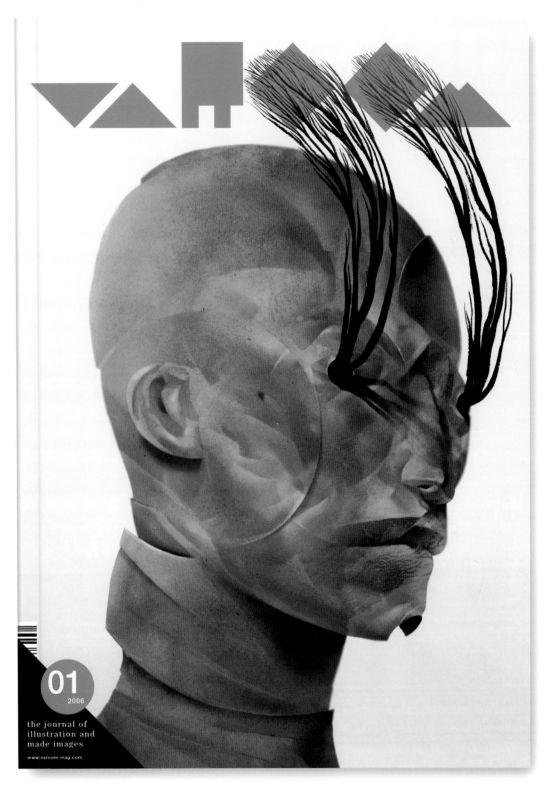

01
2006
the journal of
illustration and
made images
www.varoom-mag.com

Index of illustrators

Jill Calder 99
10 John Street
Cellardyke
Fife
KY10 3BB
Scotland
T 01333 313 737
M 07881 520 662
E jill@jillcalder.com
W www.jillcalder.com

Tony Campbell 155
A Private View (PVUK)
17a Swan Hill
Shrewsbury
SY1 1NL
T 01743 350 355
F 01743 233 923
E create@pvuk.com
W www.pvuk.com

Rebecca Canavan 258
M 07985 691 042
E rebeccacanavan@yahoo.co.uk

Graham Carter 80-81
A Private View (PVUK)
17a Swan Hill
Shrewsbury
SY1 1NL
T 01743 350 355
F 01743 233 923
E create@pvuk.com
W www.pvuk.com

Leslie Carter 218
9 Dale Avenue
Heswall
Wirral
CH60 7TA
T 0151 342 6425
M 07746 356 584
E lierbag@btopenworld.com
W www.lookspromising.co.uk

Frances Castle 129
53c Finsbury Park Road
London
N4 2JY
T 020 7288 1271
M 07876 364 945
E frances.castle@btinternet.com
W www.smallmoonvalley.com

John Charlesworth 138
72 Frost Street
Ettingshall
Wolverhampton
Staffordshire
WV2 2LL
T 01902 498 308
E jc@johncharlesworth.com
W www.johncharlesworth.com
A Neil Rogers
Between Beautiful (UK Agent)
21c Montpelier Row
Blackheath
London
T 020 8297 5235
E info@betweenbeautiful.com
W www.betweenbeautiful.com

Nishant Choksi 31
M 07855 362 694
E nish@nishantchoksi.com
W www.nishantchoksi.com

Eleanor Clark 144-145
4 Kendrick Mews
London
SW7 3HG
T 020 7225 2374
M 07939 231 066
E mail@eleanorclark.com
W www.eleanorclark.com
A Folio
10 Gate Street
Lincolin's Inn Fields
London
WC2A 3HP
T 020 7242 9562
F 020 7242 1816
E all@folioart.co.uk
W www.folioart.co.uk

Simon Clark 270
16 The Hyde
Winchcombe
Cheltenham
Gloucestershire
GL54 5QR
T 01242 602 667
M 07974 676 789
E simon@si-clark.co.uk
W www.si-clark.co.uk

Russell Cobb 37, 68-70
The Studio
St Bridgets
Radcliffe Road
Hitchin
Hertfordshire
SG5 1QH
T 01462 441 614
F 01462 441 614
M 07961 414 613
E russell@russellcobb.com
W www.russellcobb.com
A Lucy Scherer
The Artworks
40 Frith Street
London
W1D 5LN
T 020 7734 3333
F 020 7734 3483
E lucy@theartworksinc.com
W www.theartworksinc.com

Sarah Coleman 41
71 Rose Cottages
Factory Road
Hinckley
Leicestershire
LE10 0DW
T 01455 632 819
F 01455 632 819
M 07941 279 374
E sarah@inkymole.com
W www.inkymole.com

Stephen Collins 108-109
1 Beatrice Road
Norwich
Norfolk
NR1 4BB
T 01603 762 996
M 07813 065 493
E stephen.collins3@virgin.net
W www.stephencollinsillustration.com

Sarah Coulston 256
14 Campion Drive
Guisborough
Cleveland
TS14 8EU
T 01287 632 811
M 07790 415 175
E sarahcoulston@hotmail.com
W www.runonwires.co.uk

Caroline Crampton 266
260 Felixstowe Road
Ipswich
Suffolk
IP3 9AB
T 01473 271 376
E cgcrampton-illustration@yahoo.co.uk
W www.carolinecrampton.co.uk

Sara Creson 119
Upper Maisonette
119 Northchurch Road
London
N1 3NU
T +46 (0)704 500 613
M 07981 234109
E saracreson@yahoo.se

Jonathan Croft 205
T 01444 461 996
M 07944 343 365
E jonathan.croft@btinternet.com
W www.jonathancroft.com

Mel Croft 53
T 01444 461 996
M 07939 037 239
E mel.croft@btinternet.com
W www.melcroft.biz
A Eyecandy
T 020 8291 0729

Brian Cronin 105
New York City
New York
USA
T +1 212 727 9539
E brian@briancronin.com
W www.briancronin.com

Julian Crouch 203
6 Mountbatten House
Hillcrest
North Road
London N6 4HJ
M 07779 265 394
E juliancrouch@mac.com
W www.juliancrouch.com

Jonathan Cusick 170-171
10 Wynyates
Sageside
Tamworth
Staffordshire B79 7UP
T 0182 750 003
F 0182 750 003
E theboss@jonathancusick.com
W www.jonathancusick.com

Trina Dalziel 203
M 07909 637 236
E trina.dalziel@mail.com
W www.trinadalziel.com
A New Division
T 020 7593 0505
W www.newdivision.com
E info@newdivision.com

Nathan Daniels 148-149
Centrespace
6 Leonard Lane
Bristol
BS1 1EA
M 07833 122 476
E nathan@nathandaniels.com
W www.nathandaniels.com
A The Collective
T 01526 354 788

Nick Dewar 204
300 S Broadway
No.6 L Tarrytown
New York
10591 USA
T +1 914 332 1042
F +1 914 332 1042
E nick.dewar@verizon.net
A Andrea Plummer
Eastwing
99 Chase Side
Enfield
London
EN2 6NL
T 020 8367 6760
F 020 8367 6730
E andrea@eastwing.co.uk
W www.eastwing.co.uk

Ian Dodds 62-64
18 Ramsey Close
Rubery
Rednal
Birmingham
B45 0HQ
M 07905 243 739
E contact@iandodds.co.uk
W www.iandodds.co.uk

Barry Downard 94
A Andrew Coningsby
Debut Art
30 Tottenham Street
London
W1T 4RJ
T 020 7636 1064
F 020 7580 7017
E andrew@debutart.demon.co.uk
W www.debutart.com

Thomas Dowse 276
28 Leyton Avenue
Gillingham
Kent
ME7 3DB
M 07708 359 793
E thom1million@hotmail.co.uk

Stan Eales 94
34 Undine Street
Tooting
London
SW17 8PR
T 020 8682 1894
M 07717 762 413
E stan@staneales.freeserve.co.uk
W www.staneales.freeserve.co.uk

Ann Ellis 98
9 Medway Close
Lostock Hall
Preston
Lancs
PR5 5AF
T 07005 982 096
F 07005 982 097
E ann@annellis.co.uk
W www.annellis.co.uk

Max Ellis 96-97
60 Clonmel Road
Teddington
Middlesex
TW11 0SR
T 020 8977 8924
M 07976 242 378
E max@junkyard.co.uk
W www.junkyard.co.uk
A Central Illustration Agency (CIA)
W www.centralillustration.com

Ann Elson 120
Linden Gate
Redhill
North Somerset
BS40 5RP
T 01934 862 840
M 07884 026 210
E annieelson@aol.com
W www.annelson.me.uk
A Jessie Sim
Drawer
PO Box 330
163 Halfmoon Lane
North Dulwich
London
SE24 9WB
T 01225 445 262 / 020 7501 9106
E jps@drawer.me.uk
W www.drawer.me.uk

Gary Embury 10-11
12 Park Road
Blandford Forum
Dorset
DT11 7BX
T 01258 45 1424
M 0787 1186 447
E garyembury@talktalk.net
W www.embury.co.uk
A Abby Glassfield
The Inkshed
99 Chase Side
Enfield
EN2 6NL
T 020 8367 4545
F 020 8367 6730
E abby@inkshed.co.uk
W www.inkshed.co.uk

Michael English 95
17 Prince Of Wales Drive
Battersea
London
SW11 4SB
T 020 7228 8155

Claire Failes 275
22 Somerset Close
Kingswood
Wotton-Under-Edge
GL12 8RQ
T 01453 845 583
M 07889 563 905
E claire@drawingonreality.co.uk
W www.drawingonreality.co.uk

Anna-Louise Felstead MA(RCA) 218
12 Kirkstall House
Sutherland Street
London
SW1V 4JW
T 020 7233 8947
M 07887 714 637
E info@alfelstead.com
W www.alfelstead.com

Adam Fisher 244-245
46 Rolls Avenue
Forest Park Estate
Penpedairheol
Hengoed C.C.B
South Wales
CF8 28HP
M 07835 054 461
E adam@fisherart.co.uk
W www.fisherart.co.uk

Index of illustrators

A Agent
T Telephone
F Fax
M Mobile
E Email
W Website

To call from outside the UK add the prefix '44' and omit the first '0' from the number provided.

Index of illustrators

Nicholas Rooke   221
21 Chevallier Street
Ipswich
Suffolk
IP1 2PF
T 01473 211 271
M 07881 812 080
E info@rookieworld.com
W www.rookieworld.com

Victoria Rose   189
Attwood Farm
Gastard
Corsham
Wiltshire
SN13 9QW
T 01249 714 378
M 07866 621424
E victoria@victoriarose.me.uk
W www.victoriarose.me.uk

Salvatore Rubbino   275
85 Geere Road
London
E15 3PP
M 07985027750
E salvatore.rubbino@alumni.rca.ac.uk
A The Artworks
T 020 7734 3333
W www.theartworksinc.com

Harriet Russell   18, 224-225
Happiness at Work
1 Green Bank
Wapping
London E1W 2PA
T 020 7480 5638
M 07977 151 277
E harriet77@clara.co.uk
W www.harrietrussell.co.uk
A Central Illustration Agency (CIA)
T 020 78361106

Laura Scott   119
Tyddyn du Farmhouse
Dyffryn Ardudwy
Gwynedd
LL44 2DW
T 01341 247 203
M 07786 213 458
E laulizscott@yahoo.co.uk
A Jess Sims
Drawer
31 Arundel Road
Bath
BA1 6EF
T 01225 462 940
E jps@drawer.me.uk
W www.drawer.me.uk

Carol Seatory   71
9 Park View Terrace
Stanford Road
Brighton
East Sussex
BN1 5PW
T 01273 889 632
M 07980 690 923
E mail@carolseatory.co.uk
W www.carolseatory.co.uk

Liza Seel   267
110 Park Farm Road
Great Barr
Birmingham
B43 7QH
M 07968 361 920
E lizaseel@hotmail.com

Serge Seidlitz   34-35
A Andrew Coningsby
Debut Art
30 Tottenham Street
London
W1T 4RJ
T 020 7636 1064
E info@debutart.com
W www.debutart.com

Andrew Selby   102
25 Alsthorpe Road
Oakham
Rutland LE15 6FD
T 01572 774 357
M 07973 271 449
E andrew.selby1@virgin.net
W www.andrew-selby.com
A Illustration Ltd
T 020 7720 5202

Michael Sheehy   193
M 078145 87136
E michael.sheehy@btinternet.com
A Central Illustration Agency (CIA)
36 Wellington Street
London
WC2E 7BD
T 020 7240 8925
W www.centralillustration.com

Martyn Shouler   237-238
3 The Old Mews
Clarendon Street
Bedford
MK41 7DP
T 01234 302 561
M 07981 460 303
E martyn.shouler@ntlworld.com
W www.shouler-m.net

Benedict Siddle   262-263
67 Holmewood Gardens
Brixton
London
SW2 3NB
M 07775 710 612
E elcid4@hotmail.com

Lasse Skarbovik   54-55
Stora Nygatan 44
111 27 1182 Stockholm
SWEDEN
T +46 822 2433
M +46 707 228 567
E lasse@stockholmillustration.com
W www.stockholmillustration.com

Imogen Slater   221
M 07711 778 087
E imogen_slater@yahoo.co.uk
W www.imogenslater.com

Paul Slater   220
22 Partridge Close
Chesham
Bucks
HP5 3EH
T 01494 786 780
F 01494 792 562
E paulslater@btinternet.com
A Central Illustration Agency (CIA)
T 020 7240 8925

Andy Smith   226-227
45 Hubert Rd
East Ham
London
E6 3EX
T 020 8503 5959
M 07949 997 978
E andy@asmithillustration.com
W www.asmithillustration.com

Jim Smith   130
93A Elspeth Road
London
SW11 1DP
M 07789 376 083
E jimsmithorig@hotmail.com
W www.waldopancake.com

Spiral Studio   50
A Andrew Coningsby
Debut Art
30 Tottenham Street
London
W1 4RJ
T 020 7636 1064
F 020 7580 7017
E andrew@debutart.demon.co.uk
W www.debutart.com

Simon Stephenson   206
A NB Illustration
40 Bowling Green Lane
London
EC1R 0NE
T 020 7278 9131
F 020 7278 9121
E info@nbillustration.co.uk
W www. nbillustration.co.uk

Simon Stern   182-183
19 Corringham Road
London
NW11 7BS
T 020 8458 8250
F 020 8458 8250
E work@simonstern.fsnet.co.uk
W www.contact-me.net/simonstern
A Abby Glassfield
The Inkshed
99 Chase Side
Enfield
EN2 6NL
T 020 8367 4545
F 020 8367 6730
E work@inkshed.co.uk
W www.inkshed.co.uk

Alice Stevenson   250
42 Wilmington Avenue
London
W4 3HA
M 07915 609 743
E alicestevenson77@hotmail.co.uk
W www.alicestevenson.com

Nicholas Street   103
163 Wellfield Road
London
SW16 2BY
M 07814 684 552
E contact@nickstreet.co.uk
W www.nickstreet.co.uk

Rachel Swirles   242
Cornerways
1 High Street
Welbourn
Lincoln
LN5 0NH
T 01400 273 052
M 07752 5533 847
E rachelswirles@aol.com

Jules A. Sykes   185
Unit 1 C
Cooper House
2 Michael Road
London
SW6 2AD
T 020 8847 1640
M 07870 618 004
E jules@circa1.demon.co.uk
W www.circa1.demon.co.uk

Faye Tabone   257
14 Clifton Hill
Brighton
BN13HQ
T 01273 719 334
M 07753 292 983
E iamfaye@hotmail.com

Nahoshi Tanaka   238
6-2-5-108 Takiyama
Higashikurume-shi
Tokyo 203-0033
JAPAN
T +81 424 746 867
M 07906 334977
E nahoshi7@aol.com,
nahoshi7@yahoo.co.jp

Sharon Tancredi   196-197
45 Jersey Street
Brighton
BN2 9NU
T 01273 539 150
M 07802 481 459
E s.tancredi@btinternet.com
W www.sharontancredi.com

Des Taylor   156
A Private View (PVUK)
17a Swan Hill
Shrewsbury
SY1 1NL
T 01743 350 355
F 01743 233 923
E create@pvuk.com
W www.pvuk.com

Jay Taylor   253
59 Lingfield Drive
Great Wyrley
Walsall
Staffs
WS6 6LS
M 07845 517 349
E jaytaylor@scribblejay.co.uk
W www.scribblejay.co.uk

Daniela Jaglenka Terrazzini   163
A Stephanie Alexander
The Artworks
T 020 7734 3333
E steph@theartworksinc.com
W www.theartworksinc.com

Michelle Thompson   132
T 01799 523 229
M 07956 180 211
E michellethompson.studio@
btinternet.com
W www.contact-me.net/
michellethompson
A The Inkshed
T 020 8367 4545

Ella Tjader   137
T 0141 954 5008
M 07962 109 020
E contact@artlaundry.com
W www.artlaundry.com
A Harry Lyon-Smith
Illustration Ltd
2 Brooks Court
Cringle Street
London
SW8 5BX
T 020 7720 5202
E team@illustrationweb.com
W www.illustrationweb.com

Caroline Tomlinson   192
19B Berrymead Gardens
London
W3 8AA
T 020 3110 0107
F 020 3110 0107
M 07709 769 331
E info@carolinetomlinson.com
W www.carolinetomlinson.com

Lucille Toumi   128
66 Gileswood Crescent
Brampton Bierlow
Rotherham
S63 6BU
T 01709 760 513
M 07779 166 665
E lucilletoumi@hotmail.com
W www.lucilletoumi.co.uk

Dominic Trevett   184-185
M 077 7944 7676
E info@dominictrevett.co.uk
W www.dominictrevett.co.uk
A Andrew Coningsby
Debut Art
30 Tottenham Street
London
W1T 4RJ
T 020 7636 1064
F 020 7580 7017
E andrew@debutart.demon.co.uk
W www.debutart.com

Ted Tuesday   191
M 07762 157 459
E info@tedtuesday.com
W www.tedtuesday.com

Louise Tyers   269
M 07834 555 395
E lou_tyers@yahoo.co.uk
W www.lou-tyers-illustration.co.uk

Index of illustrators

A Agent
T Telephone
F Fax
M Mobile
E Email
W Website

To call from outside the UK add the prefix '44' and omit the first '0' from the number provided.

THE HENLEY COLLEGE LIBRARY

the AOI would like to **Thank**

templar publishing

www.templarco.co.uk

THE ARTWORKS

theguardian

287

NewScientist

www.AOIimages.com

the illustration resource for art-buyers and commissioners

Portfolios
With new images added daily, our portfolios now carry 8000 illustrations by nearly 500 artists. An in-depth search facility helps you find just the right image for your project.

Images – The Best of British Contemporary Illustration
The only jury-selected source book online. Browse recent editions.

Directory
Portal featuring direct links to the work of over 800 illustrators.

AOIimages.com has been developed by the Association of Illustrators to promote contemporary illustration to the creative industries.

illustration: Carol Del Angel